KU-754-693

The Nearest Thing to Life

JAMES WOOD

JONATHAN CAPE
LONDON

Published by Jonathan Cape 2015

3 5 7 9 10 8 6 4

Jonathan Cape, an imprint of Vintage Publishing,
20 Vauxhall Bridge Road,
London SW1V 2SA

Jonathan Cape is part of the Penguin Random House group of companies whose
addresses can be found at global.penguinrandomhouse.com.

Copyright © James Wood 2015

James Wood has asserted his right to be identified as the author of this Work in
accordance with the Copyright, Designs and Patents Act 1988

First published by Jonathan Cape in 2015

First published in the United States of America by University Press of
New England in 2015

www.vintage-books.co.uk

A CIP catalogue record for this book is available from the British Library

ISBN 9780224102049

Typeset in Sabon 11/15 pt by Palimpsest Book Production Limited,
Falkirk, Stirlingshire
Printed and bound by Clays Ltd, St Ives plc

Penguin Random House is committed to a sustainable future
for our business, our readers and our planet. This book is made from
Forest Stewardship Council® certified paper.

Contents

For C.D.M.

And in memory of Sheila
Graham Wood (1927–2014)

Art is the nearest thing to life; it is a mode of amplifying experience and extending our contact with our fellow-men beyond the bounds of our personal lot

George Eliot, 'The Natural History of German Life'

1
WHY?

I

RECENTLY, I WENT TO the memorial service of a man I had never met. He was the younger brother of a friend of mine, and had died suddenly, in the middle of things, leaving behind a wife and two young daughters. The programme bore a photograph, above his compressed dates (1968–2012). He looked ridiculously young, blazing with life – squinting a bit in bright sunlight, and smiling slightly as if he were just beginning to get the point of someone's joke. In some terrible way, his death was the notable, the heroic fact of his short life; all the rest was the usual joyous ordinariness, given testament by various speakers. Here he was, jumping off a boat into the Maine waters; here he was, as a child, larkily peeing from a cabin window with two young cousins; here he was, living in Italy and learning Italian by flirting; here he was, telling a great joke; here he was, an ebullient friend, laughing and filling the room with his presence. As is generally the case at such final celebrations, speakers struggled to expand and hold the beautifully banal instances of a life, to fill the dates between 1968 and 2012, so that we might leave the church thinking not of the first and last dates but of the dateless minutes in between.

It is an unusual and in some ways unnatural advantage to be able to survey the span of someone else's life, from start to finish. Such surveillance seems peremptory, high-handed, *forward*. Grief does not seem entitlement enough for the arrogation of the divine powers of beginning and ending. We are uneasy with such omniscience. We do not possess it with regard to our own lives, and we do not usually seek it with regard to the lives of others.

But if this ability to see the whole of a life is godlike, it also contains within itself the beginning of a revolt against God: once a life is contained, finalised, as if flattened within the pages of a diary, it becomes a smaller, contracted thing. It is just a life, one of millions, as arbitrary as everyone else's, a named tenancy that will soon become a nameless one; a life that we know, with horror, will be thoroughly forgotten within a few generations, like our own. At the very moment we play at being God, we also work against God, hurl down the script, refuse the terms of the drama, appalled by the meaninglessness and ephemerality of existence. Death gives birth to the first question – *Why?* – and kills all the answers. And how remarkable, that this first question, the word we utter as small children when we realise that life will be taken away from us, does not change, really, in depth or tone or mode, throughout our lives. It is our first and last question, uttered with the same incomprehension, grief, rage and fear at sixty as at six. Why do people die? Since people die, why do they live? What is the point of a life? Why are we here? Blanchot puts it well in one of his essays; by exaggeration he conveys the stunned truancy of the apprehension: 'Each person dies, but everyone is alive, and that really also means everyone is dead.'

The *Why?* question is a refusal to accept death, and is thus a theodicean question; it is the question that, in the long history of theology and metaphysics, has been answered – or shall we say, replied to – by theodicy, the formal term for the attempt to reconcile the suffering and the meaninglessness of life with the notion of a providential, benign and powerful deity. Theodicy is a project at times ingenious, bleak, necessary, magnificent and platitudinous. There are many ways to turn round and round the stripped screw of theological justification, from Augustine's free-will defence to the heresy of Gnosticism; from God's majestic bullying of Job (be quiet and know my unspeakable power) to Dostoevsky's realisation that there is no answer to the *Why?* question except through the love of Christ – embodied in Alyosha's kiss of his brother, and Father Zosima's saintliness. But these belong to the literary and theological tradition. The theodicean question is also being uttered every day, far from such grand or classic statements, and the theodicean answer is offered every day, too – with clumsy love, with optimistic despair, with cursory phlegm, by any parent who has had to tell a child that *perhaps* life does indeed continue in heaven, or that *God's ways are not our own*, or that Daddy and Mummy *simply don't know why such things happen*. If the theodicean question does not change throughout a lifetime, so the theodicean answers have not changed, essentially, in three millennia: God's reply to Job is as radically unhelpful as the parent who replies to little Annie's anguished questions by telling her to *be quiet and go and read a book*. All of us still live within this question and live within these fumbled answers.

When I was a child, the *Why?* question was acute, and had a religious inflection. I grew up in an intellectual household that was also a religious one, and with the burgeoning apprehension that intellectual and religious curiosity might not be natural allies. My father was a zoologist who taught at Durham University, my mother a schoolteacher at a local girls' school. Both parents were engaged Christians; my mother came from a Scottish family with Presbyterian and evangelical roots. The scriptures saturated everything. My father called my relationship with my first girlfriend 'unedifying' (though in order to deliver this baleful, Kierkegaardian news, he had to ambush me in the car, so that he could avoid catching my eye). I was discouraged from using the suspiciously secular term 'good luck', and encouraged to substitute it with the more providential 'blessing'. One was blessed to do well in school exams, blessed to have musical talent, blessed to have nice friends and, alas, blessed to go to church. My untidy bedroom, said my mother, was an example of 'poor stewardship'. Dirty laundry was somehow unchristian.

When I asked where God came from, my mother showed me her wedding ring and suggested that, like it, God had no beginning or end. (But I knew that someone had made the ring, even if I didn't say so.) When I asked about famines and earthquakes, my father told me, correctly enough, that humans were often politically responsible for the former and, in the case of the latter, were often to blame for continuing to live in notoriously unstable areas. Well, so much for remediable poverty and pestilence, but what about cancer, mental and physical handicap, awful accident, the freakish viral attack that felled my friend's brother at the age of forty-four? Why is there so *much* suffering, so *much* death? I was told that God's ways are incomprehensible and that, in many cases, a Job-like humility before the incomprehensible must be cultivated. But Job was a complainer before he was a saint or stoic, and I fear that my childish questioning got permanently jammed in the position of metaphysical complaint.

My anguish about death was keen because two members of my parents' congregation died at early ages, from cancer; one of them was a single mother. I played with her children. Prayers were uttered; prayers were unanswered – except that, when my parents told me that 'God has called Mrs Currah to be with Him in heaven', it seemed that, in some mind-bending way, God might have been answering our prayers by failing to answer our prayers.

So enquiry was welcomed up to a certain point, and discouraged as soon as it became rebellious. Job could not become Captain Ahab. This illiberality, coupled with my sense that official knowledge was somehow secretive, enigmatic, veiled – that we don't know why things are, but that *somewhere someone does* and is withholding the golden clue – encouraged, in me, countervailing habits of secrecy and enigma. I would reply to their esoterica with my esoterica, their official lies with my amateur lies. They believed that this world was fallen, but that restitution was promised elsewhere, in an afterlife. I believed that this world was fallen, and that there was no afterlife. As they kept the actuality of their afterlife a kind of prized secret, I would keep my revelation that there was no afterlife a prized secret, too. I became a formidable liar, the best I knew, accomplished and chronic. Lying went all the way down: you started by withholding the big truth, your atheism, and ended by withholding small truths – that you swore among friends, or listened to Led Zep, or had more than one drink, or still had the unedifying girlfriend.

Literature, specifically fiction, allowed an escape from these habits of concealment – partly because it offered a symmetrical analogical version of them, a world of the book within which lies (or fictions) were being used to protect meaningful truths. I still remember that adolescent thrill, that sublime discovery of the novel and short story as an *utterly free space*, where anything might be thought, anything uttered. In the novel, you might encounter atheists, snobs, libertines, adulterers, murderers, thieves, madmen riding across the Castilian plains or wandering around Oslo or St Petersburg, young men on the make in Paris, young women on the make in London, nameless cities, placeless countries, lands of allegory and surrealism, a human turned into a beetle, a Japanese novel narrated by a cat, citizens of many countries, homosexuals, mystics, landowners and butlers, conservatives and radicals, radicals who were also conservatives, intellectuals and simpletons, intellectuals who were also simpletons, drunks and priests, priests who were also drunks, the quick and the dead. There was the nice stealthiness of canonicity, whereby authors who had been approved by posterity or enshrined in university study, or simply given authority as a Penguin Modern Classic (the austere glamour of those light-grey covers – I remember my brother saying solemnly to me, as we loitered by shelves, 'If I publish a book I would want it to be done by Penguin'), turned out to be anything but respectable – turned out to be blasphemous, radical, raucous, erotic.

I would come back from the bookshop, these paperbacks glowing, irradiated by the energy of their compressed contents, seething like porn, as I slipped them past my unwitting parents and into my bedroom. Did they not know how blasphemous and riotously anti-clerical Cervantes was; or that Dostoevsky, despite his avowedly Christian intentions, was feeding my very atheism? *Lady Chatterley's Lover* was still officially a 'naughty' book, but Lawrence's earlier, beautiful novel, *The Rainbow*, had somehow escaped such censure. And yet, open the pages of that book and here were Will and Anna, in the first, gloriously erotic, swooning months of their marriage, and here was Will noticing that as his pregnant wife was nearing her due date, she was becoming rounder, 'the breasts becoming important'. And here was Anna dancing naked in her bedroom, as David once danced before the Lord; and Ursula and Skrebensky, kissing under the moon. And the marvellous scenes in which Skrebensky and Ursula run away to London and Paris – how simple and beautiful, the way Ursula, while always finding something spiritually lacking in Skrebensky, emphatically falls in love with sex and her lover's shape. In a London hotel room she watches him bathing: 'He was slender, and, to her, perfect, a clean, straight-cut youth, without a grain of superfluous body.'

It might seem a relatively tame licence, this notion that anything can be thought, anything written, that thought is utterly free. Aren't most of us exercising that licence every day, in our own minds? Why cherish fiction for merely replicating this exhausted liberty? But many of us don't exercise that liberty; we nervously step up to the edge of allowable thought, and then trigger the scrutiny of the censuring superego. And fiction adds the doubleness of all fictional life: to witness that freedom in *someone else* is to have a companion, is to be taken into the confidence of otherness. We share and scrutinise at the same time; we are and are not Raskolnikov and Mrs Ramsay and Miss Brodie and the narrator of Hamsun's *Hunger*, and Italo Calvino's Mr Palomar. This should feel exciting and also a little unseemly. Reading fiction feels radically private because so often we seem to be stealing the failed privacies of fictional characters. For sure, Shakespeare anticipates and contains all of the unruly life to be found in the modern novel. But Shakespearean soliloquy is *uttered privacy* (which has its roots in prayer, and ultimately in the psalms), while fictional stream of consciousness is, or tries to resemble, *unvoiced soliloquy*. And unvoiced soliloquy seems to meet our own unfinished thoughts, with the request that together we – the reader and the fictional character – complete, voice, a new ensemble. Their failed privacies become our more successful privacies.

The idea that anything could be thought and said inside the novel – a garden where the great *Why?* hangs unpicked, gloating in the free air – had, for me, an ironically symmetrical connection with the actual fears of official Christianity outside the novel: that without God, as Dostoevsky put it, 'everything is permitted'. Take away God, and anything will happen: chaos and confusion reign; people will commit all kinds of crimes, think all kinds of thoughts. You need God to keep a lid on things. This is the usual conservative Christian line. By contrast, the novel seems, commonsensically, to say: 'Everything has always been permitted, even when God was around. God has nothing to do with it.'

Of course, the novel's licence seems easier to inhabit than the world's, because novels are fictional worlds. Fiction is a ceaseless experiment with uncollectible data. What I loved, what I love, about fiction is its proximity to, and final difference from, religious texts. The real, in fiction, is always a matter of belief – it is up to us, as readers, to validate and confirm. It is a belief that is requested, and that we can refuse at any time. Fiction moves in the shadow of doubt, knows it is a true lie, knows that at any moment it might fail to make its case. Belief in fiction is always belief 'as if'. Our belief is metaphorical and only resembles actual belief. In his essay 'Sufferings and Greatness of Richard Wagner', Thomas Mann writes that fiction is always a matter of 'not quite'. 'To the artist, new experiences of "truth" are new incentives to the game, new possibilities of expression, no more. He believes in them, he takes them seriously, just so far as he needs to in order to give them the fullest and profoundest expression. In all that he is very serious, serious even to tears – but yet *not quite* – and by consequence, not at all.' Fiction, being the game of not quite,

12

is the place of not-quite-belief. Precisely what is a danger in religion is the very fabric of fiction.

II

How could these issues of freedom and surveillance not vibrate deeply, in a literary culture so marked by religious tradition? Jesus himself seemed unable to decide whether he was the ideal reader of fiction, or its implacable enemy. The Jesus who challenges the sinless to throw the first stone at the woman caught in adultery was apparently also the chief scourge of the thought-police, announcing that any man who looks upon a woman with lust in his heart has committed adultery. Now, to ask us to look into our hearts and defer judgement of a person, out of compassionate fellow-feeling, is a thoroughly novelistic gesture: we do it every day as readers of fiction. But to claim that thinking something is identical with doing it is thoroughly anti-novelistic: how could we read fiction if we actually believed this? Instinctively, though I couldn't yet formulate the objection, I resisted Jesus's parental surveillance of my own thought, while greedily availing myself of Jesus's powers of scrutiny. The assertion that for a man to look at a woman with adulterous thought is the same as committing adultery shocks us perhaps for two reasons: because Jesus claims that thought is action; and also because he seems to claim the power to know *what* you are thinking, the power to interpret your stray look, your free gesture, your aimless glance. He claims the power to make your private thought public. We flinch from this, as Coleridge does, in the *Biographia Literaria*, at the idea that Momus, the ancient personification of correction and fault-finding, might put a glass window in the breast of man so that his heart could be seen. (Poor Coleridge, the weak-willed opium addict, had much to fear from such magnified religious observation.)

In one obviously important way, to read fiction is to have non-actionable thoughts; we assert the humane, non-religious right to separate thinking from doing. To think freely is to insist on this separation, is a definition of secular thought. But when we peer into the thinking of an Isabel Archer or a Tommy Wilhelm, a Pnin or Miss Brodie, a Pechorin or Ricardo Reis, there is sometimes the vertiginous sensation of possessing Jesus's power, the power of religious monitoring – the power to turn inside out the pocket of someone else's private thoughts and watch the loose change of error fall incriminatingly to the ground. (Isaac Babel said that he could write a story about a woman if shown the contents of her handbag.) And yet: because these people we are standing over and peering into are fictional and not real, belong to a novel and not to life, our scrutiny is always edging away from judgement (of the moralistic kind), towards proximity, fellow-feeling, compassion, communion. We have the uncanny powers of the monitoring Jesus, but the humane insight of the forgiving Jesus, the sweet master who implied that all of us are as sinful as the woman caught in adultery.

To read the novel is to be constantly moving between secular and religious modes, between what could be called instance and form. The novel's secular impulse is towards expanding and extending life; the novel is the great trader in the shares of the ordinary. It expands the instances of our lives into scenes and details; it strives to run these instances at a rhythm close to real time. Think of the way that Henry James devotes an entire chapter, in *The Portrait of a Lady*, to the five or six hours that Isabel Archer sits in a chair, thinking about the failure of her marriage. Forty-five years later, Mrs Ramsay, in *To the Lighthouse*, will be sitting by the window, thinking about her children, about her husband, about all sorts of different things, and will forget that she is supposed to stay still, because Lily Briscoe is painting a portrait of her. Mrs Ramsay, in effect, forgets that she is at the centre of a portrait, forgets that she is at the centre of a novel, forgets that she is a heroine. This is a kind of secular forgetting: the novel is so full of its own life that human life seen under the eye of eternity – that is to say, life as death – has been carelessly banished. Death will roar back, but not yet, not now.

When the novel is in this forgetful secular mode, it wants its characters to live for ever. It cannot understand that they must die. Remember how reluctantly, and almost casually, Cervantes says farewell to his Don Quixote, who has been on his deathbed, and who has, at the last moment, renounced his knight errantry. He calls for Sancho Panza, and asks for forgiveness. 'Don't die, Señor' is Sancho's tearful response. Don Quixote makes his will, lives another three days and then, 'amidst the tears and lamentations of everybody present, gave up the ghost; by which I mean to say he died'. The poverty of the language, its near-clumsiness and refusal to expand into sentiment, is very moving, as if Cervantes himself was surprised by the event and is overcome with wordless grief at the passing of his creation.

But the novel's eternal or religious mode reminds us that life is bounded by death, that life is death-in-waiting. What makes the mode religious is that it shares the religious tendency to see life as bounded, already written – hence John Donne's characterisation of our lives, in his sermon on the Book of Job, as a sentence already written by God: 'Our whole life is but a parenthesis, our receiving of our soul, and delivering it back again, makes up the perfect sentence; Christ is Alpha and Omega, and our Alpha and Omega is all we are to consider.' In this mode, the novel does as God vouchsafes to do in Psalm 121: 'The Lord shall preserve thy going out and thy coming in.' It teaches us about the relation of instance to form. That is an achievement, because most of us find it difficult to apprehend the form of our lives. We are just getting through the instances – eating breakfast, going to work, earning a living, making sure the children get to school, and so on. Even when the instances are joyous – falling in love, say – *especially* when the instances are joyous, time goes slack and we are not able to see, in our great relaxation, the shape of our moments, their beginnings and ends, their phases and periods. We are condemned to understand our going out and coming retrospectively, as if we were rowing a boat, clear-eyed only about the distance we have already covered. I was happy in this city, we say, when we return to it years later; I was unhappy throughout my twenties; I was truly in love once; it was a mistake, I now see, to have taken that job. After attending the memorial service for the younger brother of my friend, I learned that his father had written a poem that contained this moving lament: 'that perfect summer . . . when nobody in the family was dying'.

At the service, I was struck by the thought that death gives us the awful privilege of seeing a life whole; that a funeral or even an obituary is a liturgical home for that uneasy privilege; and that fiction is the literary genre that most powerfully offers a secular version of that liturgical hospitality. I thought of Walter Benjamin's argument, in his essay 'The Storyteller', that classic storytelling is structured around death. It is, as it were, the fire at which listeners warm their hands. Death provides the storyteller's authority. It is death, says Benjamin, that makes a story transmissible. My wife, who is a novelist, wrote recently to a friend whose mother had just died: 'There is this strangeness of a life story having no shape – or more accurately, nothing but its present – until it has its ending; and then suddenly the whole trajectory is visible.' She was talking about her own experience, as someone who had witnessed, in the last two years, the death of both her parents. She went on to quote something that a Canadian novelist had said to her when her own father had died: that now he was dead, she suddenly missed him at all their ages. She missed him as he had been when she was a nine-year-old girl, and as he had been when she was a teenager, and when she was twenty-eight, and thirty-five, and so on.

The novel often gives us that formal insight into the shape of someone's life: we can see the beginning and end of many fictional lives; their developments and errors; stasis and drift. Fiction does this in many ways – by sheer scope and size (the long, peopled novel, full of many lives, many beginnings and endings) but also by compression and brevity (the novella that radically compacts a single life, from start to finish, as in *The Death of Ivan Ilyich* or Denis Johnson's *Train Dreams*, or Alice Munro's novella-like story, 'The Bear Came over the Mountain'). And partly by turning the present into past: although we move forward through a story, the entire story is already complete. We hold it in our hands. In this sense, fiction, the great life-giver, also kills – not just because people often die in novels and stories, but more importantly because, even if they do not die, *they have already happened*. Fictional form is always a kind of death, in the way that Blanchot described actual life. '*Was*. We say *he is*, then suddenly *he was*, this terrible *was*, I thought.' That is the narrator of Thomas Bernhard's novella, *The Loser*, describing his friend Wertheimer, who has committed suicide. But it might also describe the tense in which we encounter most fictional lives: we say, 'She was', not 'She is'. He left the house, she rubbed her neck, she put down her book and went to sleep.

A struggle is often going on in a novel, between present and past, instance and form, free will and determinism, secular expansion and religious contraction. This is why the role of authorial omniscience has such a fraught history: the anxiety is partly a theological one and has the unresolved nature of a theological argument. The novel seems forever unable to decide whether it wants to revel in omniscience or apologise for it, foreground it or foreclose it. Should the novelist intervene and interrupt, or withdraw into impersonality and frigid indifference? Nabokov liked to point out that his characters were his slaves; a character crossed the road because he made him do so. But who was ever fooled that the 'impersonal' Flaubertian author, with his gaze into Emma Bovary's soul, with his flat assertion that when they opened up the corpse of poor null Charles Bovary, they 'found nothing' – who ever thought this writer was any less godlike than chattily omniscient Henry Fielding, or essay-istic, moralising George Eliot?

Since these are transferred theological issues, it is little surprise that a number of modern novelists have been explicitly engaged with the question of what it means to tell a story, what it means to have divine power over someone's beginning and endings, and how a character might make a space for her own freedom, all the while under the watchful eye of both the author and the reader. Some authors deliberately use assertive powers of narra-tion to create in the readers a desire to assert a space of freedom for a character; to defend a character's freedom in the face of an author's intrusive arrangements. I am thinking of people like Vladimir Nabokov, Muriel Spark, V.S. Naipaul, W.G. Sebald, José Saramago, Danilo Kiš, Thomas Bernhard, Javier Marías, Ian McEwan, Jennifer Egan, Penelope Fitzgerald, Edward P. Jones, Alice Munro, Zadie Smith. In his great novel, *A House for Mr Biswas*, Naipaul tells the story of his father, in the character of Mr Biswas. It is an imprisoned, limited, fiercely deter-mined life, the life of a small man who never leaves the island of Trinidad, and dies young. The novel begins with a kind of obituary, the report of Mr Biswas's death, and the author oscillates between a slow, patient, comic account of Mr Biswas's life and a summary, religious account that cruelly squeezes Mr Biswas's life. 'In all Mr Biswas lived six years at The Chase, years so squashed by their own boredom and futility that at the end they could be comprehended in one glance.' This is religious time, and is belied by the novel itself, which tells us in its every comic, secular scene that Mr Biswas's life cannot be comprehended in one glance. The novel asks us to rise up against its own determinism, so that we become the kind of reader who can read Naipaul's ironies and resist them, and collude with him in making a space for Mr Biswas's comic waywardness.

In recent years, one of the most beautiful enactments of the great 'Why?', and of the novelistic movement between instance and form, has been Penelope Fitzgerald's brief book, *The Blue Flower*, published in 1995. It is a historical novel, and recounts the short life of the young man known to us as the philosopher and poet Novalis. His real name was Friedrich (Fritz) von Hardenberg, and when we first meet him in Fitzgerald's novel he is a passionate university student, fired up with the theories of Fichte. He thinks that death is not significant but only a change in condition. He thinks that we are all free to imagine what the world is like, and since we probably all imagine it differently, there is no reason to believe in the fixed reality of things. Fitzgerald constantly plays domestic life against Fritz's airy philosophical obliviousness. When he tells his future father-in-law that Fichte has explained that there is only one absolute self, one identity for all humanity, his father-in-law replies: 'Well, this Fichte is lucky . . . In this household I have thirty-two identities to consider.'

On a visit, Fritz meets a twelve-year-old girl, Sophie von Kühn. By all accounts, Sophie is a thoroughly ordinary twelve-year-old, yet the passionate Fritz decides, in just fifteen minutes, that he must marry Sophie, that 'Sophie is my heart's heart'; 'She is my wisdom.' Fritz has fixed ideas about women – they are closer to perfection than are men, despite the fact that they particularise, while men generalise. 'I've heard that before,' says the shrewd elder sister of Sophie, but 'what is wrong with particulars? Someone has to look after them.' Fitzgerald constantly suggests that there is a world of particulars, of domestic tasks like washing and chopping onions, as well as a world full of actual flesh-and-blood women, and that this is the world of the novel, whereas Fritz belongs to the more impalpable world of ideas. (Fitzgerald may be deliberately replaying the ideological and gender struggles of *To the Lighthouse*.) Fritz wants to write a novel, which he has provisionally titled 'The Blue Flower', but he has only written a few paragraphs, and it doesn't sound very good: 'I have made a list of occupations and professions, and of psychological types,' he explains. But there are no easily recognised types in Fitzgerald's novel; instances are not instances of types but instances of themselves. Perhaps Fritz is too high-flown for the novel? When he and Karoline Just discuss Goethe's novel *Wilhelm Meister's Apprenticeship*, they disagree about the death of Mignon. She was too pure for this world, says Fritz; nonsense, says Karoline firmly, Goethe killed her off because he didn't know what to do with her. Who sounds like the true novelist in this exchange?

Fitzgerald is herself a very practical novelist – she attends briskly to details and particulars; she eschews sentiment, preferring an elusive irony; her scenes are short, playful, exact. But she has Muriel Spark's ability to open up abysses. An example. Fritz, who is not living at home, has asked his mother, Auguste, to meet him in the garden. He wants to discuss whether his father is likely to bless his marriage to the very young and socially modest Sophie. His mother has not been alone in the garden for years, and never without her husband's permission. But she secretly gets the key to the garden gate, and meets her son.

> An extraordinary notion came to the Freifrau Auguste, that she might take advantage of this moment, which in its half-darkness and fragrance seemed to her almost sacred, to talk to her eldest son about herself. All that she had to say could be put quite shortly: she was forty-five, and she did not see how she was going to get through the rest of her life. Abruptly Fritz leaned towards her and said: 'You know that I have only one thing to ask. Has he read my letter?'

That is all Fitzgerald gives us of the inside of Auguste's mind. Of course, excitable Fritz is not aware of this feeling, and leans towards her, egotistical and insistent. It would be hard to offer a better example of what the novel can do than this moment of four sentences: the shocking, vertiginous intimacy of the revelation, and then the closing up of that intimacy, as life simply goes on.

The Blue Flower is full of that ongoing life, caught in the most delicate way. There is Fritz, and his more stolid brother Erasmus, and their sweet sister Sidonie, and the wonderful, brilliant youngest child, known by his nickname of 'The Bernhard'. But this happy family life is haunted, stalked by death. The book ends with this remarkable report:

> At the end of the 1790s, the young Hardenbergs, in their turn, began to go down, almost without protest, with pulmonary tuberculosis. Erasmus, who had insisted that he coughed blood only because he laughed too much, died on Good Friday, 1797. Sidonie lasted until the age of twenty-two. At the beginning of 1801 Fritz, who had been showing the same symptoms, went back to his parents' house in Weissenfels. As he lay dying he asked Karl to play the piano for him. When Friedrich Schlegel arrived Fritz told him that he had entirely changed his plan for the story of the Blue Flower.
>
> The Bernhard was drowned in the Saale on the 28th of November 1800.

It is a perfectly judged and weighted passage – from the apparent insouciance of the phrase 'began to go down, almost without protest', which makes death sound like a family game of musical chairs, to Erasmus's heartbreaking claim that he coughed blood only because he laughed too much (which continues the memory of family fun), to Fritz's unfinished plan to rewrite his unfinishable novel; to the blank, colourless, uninflected sentence: 'The Bernhard was drowned in the Saale on the 28th of November 1800.' The genius of the family, the one who might have been much greater than Novalis, was only twelve years old.

As her epigraph, Fitzgerald uses a line of Novalis's: 'Novels arise out of the shortcomings of history.' Indeed, her novel tries to rescue those private moments that history would never have been able to record, private moments that even a family itself might not record. But these secular instances exist within the larger, severe form of the book, which is the knowledge that these are short lives, condemned lives, nothing more than historical parentheses.

Fiction manages the remarkable feat of allowing us both to expand and contract the parenthesis. This tension, between secular instance and religious form, is acute in fiction as it is not in religious narrative; is perhaps the novel's claim to power: it's the reason the novel throws us so often into the wide, sceptical, terrifying freedom of the 'Why?' That question is powerfully mobilised by novelistic form: not just because the novel is so good at evoking the ordinary instances of a life, but because it is so good at asserting the finished, completed form of a life. By 'asserting,' I mean that because the characters we are reading about are invented, they *did not have to die*. They died because their author made them die. We feel this even in an historical novel like *The Blue Flower*, which novelises actual, historical lives. The classical historian Robin Lane Fox once commented that there is only one accidental death in the Old Testament, implying a difference from modern accounts of accidental lives and deaths offered by novels and newspaper stories. But if 'accidental' means 'unintended', then strictly speaking there are no accidental deaths in fiction. That is so even in historical fiction, because, theoretically, the novelist has the power to change history, and because the novelist has selected this character for the nature of his death as well as of his life. Besides, when we read historical fiction the characters take on lives of their own, and begin to detach themselves in our minds from the actuality of the historical record. When characters in historical novels die, they die as fictional characters, not as historical personages.

Yet fiction remains the game of not quite. Characters do *not quite* die. They come back to us – there they are, in that novel again, the second or third time we read it. The laugh of fictional life lasts longer than the bloody cough of death. One of the 'shortcomings of history' is that real people die. But fiction gives us allowable resurrections, repeated secular returns. Italo Calvino seems to play with this fictive death sentence and resurrection at the end of his novel *Mr Palomar*, when he ironically considers the death of his eponymous protagonist:

> A person's life consists of a collection of events, the last of which could also change the meaning of the whole, not because it counts more than the previous ones but because once they are included in a life, events are arranged in an order that is not chronological but rather corresponds to an inner architecture.

Mr Palomar would like to learn how to be dead, and Calvino reminds us that he will find this difficult, because the hardest thing about being dead is realising that one's own life is 'a closed whole, all in the past, to which nothing can be added'. Mr Palomar, adds Calvino, begins to imagine the end of all human existence, of time itself. 'If time has to end, it can be described, instant by instant,' Mr Palomar thinks, 'and each instant expands so that its end can no longer be seen. He decides that he will set himself to describing every instant of his life, and until he has described them all he will no longer think about being dead. At that moment he dies,' writes Calvino.

It is the last sentence of the book.

2

SERIOUS NOTICING

I

FOR THE LAST TWENTY years or so, I have returned again and again to a remarkable story, written by Anton Chekhov when he was twenty-seven. It's called 'The Kiss'. A regiment of soldiers has been billeted in a provincial town. The owner of the town's biggest house invites the officers to tea and a ball. One of them, a naïve staff-captain named Ryabovich, does not find it as easy as his confident peers to dance with the women. He is 'a short, round-shouldered officer in spectacles and with whiskers like a lynx's'. He watches his fellow-officers talk easily and flirtatiously with the women.

> In the whole of his life he had never once danced, nor had he ever put his arm round the waist of a respect-able woman . . . There was a time when he envied the confidence and go of his comrades and suffered mental anguish; the awareness that he was timid, round-shouldered and drab, that he had lynx-like

whiskers and no hips, hurt him profoundly, but with the passing of the years he had become inured to this, so that now, as he looked at his comrades dancing or conversing loudly, he no longer experienced envy, only a feeling of wistful admiration.

To hide his embarrassment and boredom, he goes wandering in the large house and gets lost, ending up in a dark room. Here, writes Chekhov, 'as in the ball-room, the windows were wide open and there was a scent of poplar, lilac, and roses'. Suddenly, behind him, he hears rushed footsteps. A woman approaches and kisses him. They both gasp, and both instantly realise that she has kissed the wrong man; she quickly retreats. Ryabovich returns to the ballroom, his hands shaking. Something has happened to him.

His neck, which had just been embraced by soft fragrant arms, seemed to have been bathed with oil; at the spot on his cheek by his left moustache where the unknown woman had kissed him, there was a slight, pleasant, cold tingling, such as you get from peppermints, and the more he rubbed the spot, the more pronounced this tingling became, whilst the whole of him, from top to toe, was filled with a new, peculiar feeling that grew and grew . . . He felt he wanted to dance, run into the garden, laugh out loud . . .

The incident grows in size and importance in the young soldier's mind. He has never kissed a woman before. In the ballroom he looks at each of the women in turn, and convinces himself that *she* was the one. That night, when he goes to bed, he has the sensation that 'someone had been kind to him and made him happy, that something unusual, absurd, but extremely good and full of joy, had taken place in his life'.

The next day the regiment breaks camp and moves on. Ryabovich cannot stop thinking about the kiss, and a few days later, at dinner, while his fellow-officers are chatting and reading the newspapers, he summons the courage to tell his story. He does tell it, and a minute later falls silent. Because it only took a minute to tell. And Ryabovich is amazed, writes Chekhov, 'to find that the story had taken such a short time. He had thought he could go on talking about the kiss all night.' To add to the sense of failure, his fellow-officers seem either bored by his short tale or sceptical of its veracity. Eventually the regiment returns to the town where the event took place. Ryabovich hopes for another invitation to the big house. But it doesn't happen, and he wanders down to a river near the house, feeling cynical and disillusioned. There are some sheets hanging over the rail of the bridge, 'and for no good reason' he touches one of the sheets. 'How absurd! . . . How stupid it all is!' he thinks, as he gazes at the water.

There are two absolutely lancing sentences in this story: 'In that minute he had told it all and was quite amazed

33

to find that the story had taken such a short time. He had thought he could go on talking about the kiss all night.'

What a *serious noticer* a writer must be to write those lines. Chekhov appears to notice everything. He sees that the story we tell in our heads is the most important one, because we are internal expansionists, comic fantasists. For Ryabovich, his story has grown bigger and bigger, and has joined, in real time, the rhythm of life. Chekhov sees that Ryabovich, painfully, does and doesn't need an audience for his story. Perhaps Chekhov is also jokily suggesting that, unlike Chekhov, the captain wasn't much of a storyteller. For there is the inescapable irony that Chekhov's own story, while taking a bit longer than a minute to tell, does not take all evening to read: like many of his tales, it is brisk and brief. Had Chekhov told it, people would have listened. Yet Chekhov also suggests that even the story we have just read – Chekhov's brief story – is not the whole account of Ryabovich's experience; that just as Ryabovich failed to tell it all, so perhaps Chekhov has not told it all. There is still the enigma of *what* Ryabovich wanted to say.

'The Kiss' is a story about a story, and reminds us that one definition of a story might be that it always produces more of them. A story is story-producing. There is Chekhov's tale; there is the discrete incident that befalls Ryabovich; and there is the untold, bottomless story that Ryabovich makes, and fails to make, of that incident. No single story can ever explain itself: this enigma at the heart of story is itself a story. Stories produce offspring, genetic splinters of themselves, hapless embodiments of their original inability to tell the whole tale.

Stories are *dynamic combinations of surplus and disappointment*: disappointing because they must end, and disappointing because they cannot really end. You might say that the surplus *is* the exquisite disappointment. A real story is endless, but it disappoints because it is begun and ended not by its own logic but by the coercive form of the storyteller: you can feel the pure surplus of life trying to get beyond the death which authorial form imposes. The story Ryabovich would ideally tell, the one that would take all evening and not a mere minute, might be the whole story of his life – something like the tale Chekhov has been telling us, though doubtless much longer and less shapely. It would not just recount the incident in the dark room, but might tell us about Ryabovich's shyness, his innocence of women, his sloping shoulders and lynx-like whiskers. It might recount things not mentioned by Chekhov, the kinds of episodes that a novel might find room for – his parents (how his father bullied him, and his mother indulged him); how his decision to become a soldier was undertaken partly to please his father, and was never something Ryabovich wanted to do; how he dislikes and rather envies his fellow-officers; how he writes poetry in his spare time, but has never shared a single line with anyone; how he dislikes his lynx-like whiskers, but needs them because they obscure an area of pitted skin.

But just as Ryabovich's one-minute story is not really worth telling, is not really a story, so the shapeless story that would take all evening is too shapeless, is not enough of a story, either. Ryabovich, one suspects, needs a Chekhovian eye for detail, the ability to notice well and seriously, the genius for selection. Do you think that Ryabovich mentioned, when he told his tale to his fellow-soldiers, that the darkened room smelt of lilac, poplar and roses? Do you think that Ryabovich mentioned that when the woman kissed him, his cheek glowed, as if brushed with peppermint? For details represent those moments in a story where form is outlived, cancelled, evaded. I think of details as nothing less than bits of life sticking out of the frieze of form, imploring us to touch them. Details are not, of course, just *bits of life*: they represent that magical fusion, wherein the maximum amount of literary artifice (the writer's genius for selection and imaginative creation) produces a simulacrum of the maximum amount of non-literary or actual life, a process whereby artifice is then indeed *converted into* (*fictional, which is to say, new*) *life*. Details are not lifelike but irreducible: things-in-themselves, what I would call lifeness itself. The detail about the peppermint, like the tingle felt by Ryabovich on his cheek, lingers for us: all we have to do is rub the spot.

Henry Green's novel *Loving* (1945) is set in an Anglo-Irish country house, and deals largely with the lives of its cockney servants. There is a moment in that book not unlike Chekhov's 'The Kiss' (and Green was a keen student of Chekhov), when the young housemaid, Edith, enters the room of her mistress, Mrs Jack, to open the curtains and bring the morning tea. Edith gets a shock, because Mrs Jack is in bed with Captain Davenport, who is not her husband. As Captain Davenport quickly disappears under the sheets, Mrs Jack sits upright, naked, and Edith runs from the room. She had seen, writes Green in a memorable phrase, 'that great brilliant upper part of' Mrs Jack, 'on which, wayward, were two dark upraised dry wounds shaking on her'. Edith is shocked but secretly thrilled – partly because it happened to her and not anyone else; partly because, for an innocent young woman, the witnessing of this scene is an initiation, at one remove, into the glamour of adult sexual relations (though Green doesn't tell us this explicitly); partly because it's something to wield in her encounters with Charley Raunce, the butler, with whom she has been increasingly flirtatious.

As in Ryabovich's case, Edith's story is intensely valuable to her, a treasure to be both hoarded and haplessly given away. 'Well then isn't this a knock out,' she crows to Charley Raunce. 'An' it happened to me . . . after all these years.' Charley, always cautious when Edith seems to be one erotic step ahead of him, is not as happy as she is. 'Well, aren't you glad?' she asks, insistently. 'You're going to try and take that from me?'

> Why [she continues] there's all those stories you've had, openin' this door and seeing that when you were in a place in Dorset and lookin' through the bathroom window in Wales an' suchlike . . . and now it's come to me. Right a'bed they was next to one another. Stuff that in your old smelly pipe and smoke it.

When Raunce tries to dismiss the singularity of Edith's experience, by claiming that the former butler, Mr Eldon, also caught Mrs Jack and her lover in bed, Edith bursts out in splendid indignation: 'D'you stand there an' tell me Mr Eldon had come upon them some time? Just as I did? That she sat up in bed with her fronts bobblin' at him like a pair of geese the way she did to me?' It's a beautiful outburst: you don't easily forget that brilliant, almost Shakespearean neologism, 'fronts', or the idea of breasts bobbling like a pair of geese.

Detail is always *someone*'s detail. Henry Green's own diction is eloquent, lyrical and sharply particular. As the literary author, as the modernist author in the third person, he describes Mrs Jack's breasts as 'dry upraised wounds'. I think he means nothing sinister by this. Like a good painter, he is getting us to look harder than we usually do at a nipple – the way the darker skin around it can look like tender scar tissue (hence 'wounds'). But Edith makes the story her own by seeing *her* details, using her words and similes. Isn't there a moving quality of desperation about Edith's need to keep the story hers?

She fears that Raunce will take it away from her, she wants her story to be the equal of Mr Raunce's stories from Dorset and Wales; and the very force of her language seems an attempt to ensure that whatever Mr Eldon saw, he did not see what *she* saw, because he did not see it as vividly and pungently as she did.

Like Ryabovich and Edith, we are the sum of our details. (Or rather, our details exceed the sum of our details; we fail to compute.) The details *are* the stories; stories in miniature. As we get older, some of those details fade, and others, paradoxically, become more vivid. We are, in a way, all internal fiction writers and poets, rewriting our memories.

I find that my memory is always yeasting up, turning one-minute moments into loafing, ten-minute reveries. Displacement also adds its own difficulties. I sometimes feel, for instance, that I grew up not in the 1970s and '80s but in the 1870s and '80s. I doubt I would feel this if I still lived in Britain, but the vanishing of certain habits and traditions, and my leaving that country for the United States in 1995, combine to make my childhood seem ridiculously remote. Often, in conversation in the States, I'm about to start a story about some aspect of my childhood, some memory, and I stop, aware that I can't quite heave into narrative the incommunicable mass of obscure and distant detail. I would have to explain too much – and then I would not have a story, would not have details, but explication; or my story would have to begin too early and end too late: it would take all evening to tell.

I was born in 1965, and grew up in a northern English town, Durham, home to a university, a majestic Romanesque cathedral and surrounded by coalfields, many of them now abandoned. Every house had a hearth and fire, and coal, rather than wood, was used as domestic fuel. Every few weeks, a lorry arrived, piled with lumpy burlap sacks; the coal was then poured down a chute into the house's cellar – I vividly remember the volcanic sound, as it tumbled into the cellar, and the drifting, blueish coal-dust, and the dark, small men who carried those sacks on their backs, with tough leather pads on their shoulders.

I went to school in Durham, an ecclesiastical institution strong in subjects like Latin, history and music. I sang in the cathedral choir, a kind of glorious indentured servitude – we performed evensong every day, and three services on Sundays. Every afternoon, we lined up in two equal columns, to walk from the school to the cathedral – dressed in thick black capes that were clasped at the neck, and black mortar boards with frondy purple tassels. The dormitories were so cold in the morning that we learned how to dress in bed. The school's headmaster, the Reverend Canon John Grove, was probably only in his early fifties, but seemed to us a fantastically antique figure. He was a bachelor and a clergyman, and wore the uniform of his calling: a black suit, a black buttonless shirt, a thick white clerical collar. (In a poem by the Scottish poet

Robin Robertson, whose father was a minister, there is the wonderful detail that his father's clerical collar was a strip of white plastic cut from a bottle of washing-up liquid.) Except for the band of white starch round his neck, Canon Grove was entirely colourless – his ancient Oxford shoes were black, his thick spectacles were black, the pipe he smoked was black. He seemed to have been carbonised centuries ago, turned into ash, and when he lit his pipe, it seemed as if he was lighting himself. Like all children, we were fascinated by the match held over the pipe-bowl, by the flame steadily journeying along the flimsy match, entranced by the sucking noises of the smoker, and the way the flame halted its horizontal passage at these moments and then briefly disappeared vertically into the bowl. And always there was the question: how can he hold the match alight for so long, with such reptilian imperviousness?

This headmaster was quite a kind soul, in his way, but he stuck to the codes of punishment he understood. Boys guilty of major sins were given 'six of the best', six hard, stinging smacks on the arse, with the back of a large, flat, wooden hairbrush. By the time I left this school, at the age of thirteen, I was triumphant about how many 'whacks' of the hairbrush I had accumulated – 106, to be precise. It seems a measure of this *pastness* that when I announced this enormous sum to my parents, they had no impulse to complain about the school and merely enquired, mildly, 'Whatever have you been up to?' There were marvellous teachers – a Latin master who said that we should begin our essays 'with a bang, as Bacon began his essay on gardens: "God Almighty first planted a garden." Try to emulate Bacon.' A history teacher who strode into class one day, took off his black gown and tossed it onto his table, upended the contents of a wastepaper bin onto that table, then proceeded to take the contents of a boy's desk and hurl them onto that table, at which point he stood behind it and grandly declaimed: 'In 1482, England was in a mess!'

Sometimes, at home, I found a tramp sitting in a chair in the kitchen, drinking a cup of tea and eating a sandwich my mother had made for him. Tom came every so often for a bite to eat before hitting the road again. He was epileptic, and once had a fit while in our kitchen, rocking back and forth, his eyes tightly closed, his hands twisting the dirty cloth of his trousers. Many years later, poor man, he fell into a fire while having a fit, and died. He had never been on a train, a fact that riveted me when I was a little boy. He had almost no concept of London, or even of the south of England. When I eventually went away down south, to university, Tom, who liked stamps, asked me to bring back any I might find, as if the south of England were a foreign country.

The cathedral is still there – massive, grey, long, solemn – but much of the rest of that world has disappeared. The coalfields were already in serious decline when I was growing up, and most of the collieries had already closed.

Coal is no longer as potent or as popular – or as native – as it once was in England. Of course, this also means that fewer men go underground to hack at coal-seams in dangerous conditions, as Orwell described so vividly in *The Road to Wigan Pier*. Fortunately, striking a child's bottom with a hard object is no longer considered an appropriate punishment; there probably isn't a school in Britain where systematic corporal punishment is still allowed, an astonishingly rapid development that began almost as soon as I entered my teens. And I doubt that tramps come round for sandwiches and tea – though they certainly still go somewhere for sandwiches and tea. When I describe this world to my twelve-year-old daughter and ten-year-old son, I seem to grow whiskers and a frock coat: they stare with amused eyes at a father now absurdly prehistoric. They live in a much gentler but oddly sanitised world, in which the only discipline at school seems to be a murmured 'time out' from the teacher, and illnesses like epilepsy happen out of sight. No one smokes much, certainly not teachers, and pipes are known only from old movies and photographs.

Of course, I don't want my children to have exactly the same childhood as I did: that would almost be a definition of conservatism. But I would like them to be assaulted by the pungency, by the vivid strength and strangeness of *detail*, that I was as a child; and I want them to notice and remember. (I'm also aware that worrying about lack of pungency is a peculiarly middle-class, Western affliction; much of the world is full of people

43

suffering from a surfeit of bloody pungency.) The carbonised clergyman; dressing in bed; Tom sitting by the kitchen
drinking his sweet tea; the coal-men with their leather
jackets – you have your equivalent details, the whatness
or thisness of your own stories.

Here is a paragraph by the Bosnian-American writer
Aleksandar Hemon. It is from his story, 'Exchange of
Pleasant Words', about a drunken and exuberant family
reunion – what the family calls a Hemoniad – in rural
Bosnia. The viewpoint is that of a teenager, close to the
ground, and drunk:

> The noxious, sour manure stench coming from the
> pigsty; the howling of the only piglet left alive; the
> fluttering of fleeting chickens; pungent smoke coming
> from moribund pig-roast fires; relentless shuffling and
> rustling of the gravel on which many feet danced; my
> aunts and other auntly women trodding the *kolomiyka*
> on the gravel, their ankles universally swollen, and
> their skin-hued stockings descending slowly down their
> varicose calves; the scent of a pine plank and then
> prickly coarseness of its surface, as I laid my head on
> it and everything spun, as if I were a washing machine;
> my cousin Ivan's sandaled left foot tap-tapping on the
> stage, headed by its rotund big toe; the vast fields of
> cakes and pastries arrayed on the bed (on which my
> grandmother had expired), meticulously sorted in
> chocolate and non-chocolate phalanxes.

Hemon, who left his native Sarajevo in 1992 and now lives in Chicago, loves lists – and when he has such good inherited material, why wouldn't he? Notice, in particular, 'the howling of the only piglet left alive', and the phalanxes of cakes and pastries arrayed on the *same bed* that the grandmother has expired on.

In ordinary life, we don't spend very long looking at things or at the natural world or at people, but writers do. It is what literature has in common with painting, drawing, photography. You could say, following John Berger, that civilians merely see, while artists look. In an essay on drawing, Berger writes that 'To draw is to look, examining the structure of experiences. A drawing of a tree shows, not a tree, but a tree being looked at. Whereas the sight of a tree is registered almost instantaneously, the examination of the sight of a tree (a tree being looked at) not only takes minutes or hours instead of a fraction of a second, it also involves, derives from, and refers back to, much previous experience of looking.' Berger is saying two things, at least. First, that just as the artist takes pains – and many hours – to examine that tree, so the person who looks hard at the drawing, or reads a description of a tree on the page, learns how to take pains, too; learns how to change seeing into looking. Second, Berger seems to argue that every great drawing of a tree has a relation to every previous great drawing of a tree, since artists learn by both looking at the world and by looking at what other artists have done with the world. Our looking is always mediated by other representations of looking.

Berger doesn't mention literary examples. But in the novel, think of the famous tree in *War and Peace*, which Prince Andrei rides past first in early spring, and then, a month later, in late spring. On his second journey, Andrei doesn't recognise the tree, because it is so changed. Before, it had been leafless and wintry. Now, it is in full bloom, surrounded by other trees similarly alive: 'Juicy green leaves without branches broke through the stiff, hundred-year-old bark, and it was impossible to believe that this old fellow had produced them.' Prince Andrei notices the tree in part because he too has changed: its healthy blossoming is related to his own.

Seventy or so years later, in his novel *Nausea*, Jean-Paul Sartre surely has in mind Tolstoy's two tree descriptions when he has his protagonist, Antoine Roquentin, experience the pivotal epiphany of the novel while looking at and thinking about a tree. When Roquentin looks at his tree, he brings to it his own speculative habits. He looks very hard at this chestnut, and especially at its roots: the bark, black and blistered, looks like boiled leather, he feels. He sees its 'compact sea-lion skin . . . that oily, horny, stubborn look', and he likens the curve of the root as it enters the ground to a 'big, rugged paw'. The epiphany that Roquentin has is an early version of Sartrean existentialism: he feels that the tree, like everything in the park, including himself, is absolutely superfluous, and has no necessity.

What is more interesting, perhaps, than his philosophy is his revelation: that what exists is simply there – what exists 'lets itself be *encountered*, but you can never *deduce* it' (Sartre's italics). As long as he has this revelation, 'I *was* the root of the chestnut tree. Or rather I was all consciousness of its existence. Still detached from it – since I was conscious of it – and yet lost in it, nothing but it.' And when, later, he tries to formulate the philosophical conclusion from this visionary moment, he notices that he is struggling with words, whereas when he stood under the tree 'he touched the thing . . . That root . . . existed in so far that I could not explain it.' On the one hand, this experience of looking at things is intensely self-conscious – for if the drawing of a tree is not a tree but 'a tree being looked at', then the verbal description of a tree is not a tree but 'a tree being looked at being described'. This is the formal, or theoretical, side of surplus. But on the other hand, the tree is also pure detail for both Andrei and Roquentin – it is nothing but a tree; it exists, as Sartre puts it, in so far as it *cannot be explained*. We are detached from details, says Sartre (because they are not identical to us); but we are also – paradoxically – nothing but these details (a tree, its bark, its roots, and so on), as Andrei and the tree are one and the same. This irreducibility is the other aspect of the life-surplus I am trying to define: the enigmatic side of surplus. Just as detail is both intensely self-conscious and intensely self-annulling, so detail, as I suggested earlier,

47

is both high artifice (the self-conscious exercise of creative power) and the magical opposite of artifice (lifeness; what Sartre calls 'the thing'). Karl Ove Knausgaard, a writer greatly engaged in the project of simultaneously describing and analysing detail does his own version of Tolstoy's and Sartre's descriptions, in a magnificent page-long sketch of a tree in Volume Three of *My Struggle*:

It was strange how all large trees had their own personalities, expressed through their unique forms and the aura created by the combined effects of the trunk and roots, the bark and branches, the light and shadow. It was as if they could speak. Not with voices, of course, but with what they were, they seemed to *stretch* out to whoever looked at them. And that was all they spoke about, what they were, and nothing else. Wherever I went on the estate or in the surrounding forest, I heard these voices, or felt the impact these extremely slow-growing organisms had.

II

What is *serious noticing*? In Saul Bellow's novella *Seize the Day*, Tommy Wilhelm, who is in his forties, helps an old man, Mr Rappaport, across the street. He takes him by the arm, and is struck by the man's 'big but light elbow'. It might not seem the most extraordinary piece of writing, but consider for a moment the precision of the paradox – the bone of the elbow is large because the old man is skinny and gnarled; but it is unexpectedly light, because Mr Rappaport is *just* skin and bone, and is gradually disappearing into his own longevity. I like to imagine the youngish writer sitting at his manuscript in 1955 or so, and trying to imagine (or perhaps remembering and imagining) the exact experience of holding an aged elbow in his hand: '*big . . . big but . . . big but light!*'

In the same novel, Tommy Wilhelm is running through the health club of a hotel, looking for his elderly father, who is getting a massage. As he rushes from room to room, he briefly catches sight of two men playing ping-pong; they have just come out of the steam-bath and are wearing towels round their waists: 'They were awkward and the ball bounded high.' Again, imagine that youngish writer at his desk. He sees, in his mind's eye, his protagonist running from room to room; he sees his protagonist notice the two men in their towels. Often with great writers, it is instructive to stop at the point in a sentence, or in a metaphor, or in a perception, where the ordinary writer might come to a halt. The ordinary writer might have Tommy Wilhelm catch sight of the two men playing ping-pong and leave it at that. ('Two men in towels were playing ping-pong.') Bellow will not leave it at that. He sees that the men are made awkward by their towels, and that, as a consequence, they are playing ineptly.

Fearful that their towels will slip, they are just pretending to play – and so 'the ball bounded high'.

Just as great writing asks us to look more closely, it asks us to participate in the transformation of the subject through metaphor and imagery. Think of the way D.H. Lawrence describes, in one of his poems, the 'drooping Victorian shoulders' of a kangaroo; or how Aleksandar Hemon (again) describes horse-shit as looking like 'dark, deflated, tennis balls', or how Elizabeth Bishop describes a taxi meter staring at her 'like a moral owl', or how the novelist and poet Adam Foulds notices a blackbird 'flinching' its way up a tree. The critic Christopher Ricks once proposed that a fairly good test of literary quality is if a sentence or image or phrase of a writer comes to your mind unbidden when you are, say, just walking down the street. But you might also be standing in front of a tree. And if you should see a bird climbing the trunk of a tree, you will see indeed that it *flinches its way up*. Speaking of streets, right now the street I live on is being dug up. New sewers are being laid, a project that has already taken months. Each day, there is much drilling, digging, opening up of the ground; and then towards mid-afternoon the workmen patch the holes with metal plates, or with gravel, so that cars can drive over them. The next day the whole process begins again, with full Promethean horror. At least four times a week I think of Nabokov's great defamiliarising joke in *Pnin*, about how the workmen come back day after day to the same spot in the road, to try to find the lost tool they accidentally entombed.

In fiction, of course, a good deal of apparently external noticing is simultaneously internal noticing – as is the case when Prince Andrei looks at the tree, or when Anna Karenina, famously, notices the size of her husband's ears, after her encounter on the train with Vronsky. Her noticing is itself noticeable, worthy of our notice, because it tells us something about her transformation. John Berger's phrase, 'examining the structure of experiences', nicely applies to this internal, or double, aspect of novelistic noticing. For fiction's chief difference from poetry and painting and sculpture – from the other arts of noticing – is this internal psychological element. In fiction, we get to examine the self in all its performance and pretence, its fear and secret ambition, its pride and sadness. It is by noticing people seriously that you begin to understand them; by looking harder, more sensitively, at people's motives, you can look around and behind them, so to speak. Fiction is extraordinarily good at dramatising how contradictory people are. How we can want two opposed things at once: think of how brilliantly Dostoevsky catches this contradiction, how we love and hate at the same time, or how quickly our moods, like clouds on a windy day, scud from one shape to another.

Often, in life, I have felt that an essentially novelistic understanding of motive has helped me to begin to fathom what someone else really wants from me, or from another person. Sometimes, it is almost frightening to realise how poorly most people know themselves; it seems to put one at an almost priestly advantage over people's souls. This is another way of suggesting that in fiction we have the great privilege of seeing how people make themselves up – how they construct themselves out of fictions and fantasies and then choose to repress or forget that element of themselves.

I've mentioned Dostoevsky's characters, who go back to the eighteenth-century Diderot, and to Lermontov's great hero, Pechorin (late 1830s), and forward to the narrator of Thomas Bernhard's novel *The Loser*, a wonderful book narrated by a man who is convinced that his friend, a pianist named Wertheimer, who has committed suicide, was 'a loser'. The narrator means by that word (*Der Untergeher* is the German title, which means one who is drowning or sinking – 'going under') that when he and Wertheimer were young, they were both desperate to be great pianists. They studied with Glenn Gould, and deeply envied Gould's pianistic genius. By comparison with Gould, who of course 'made it' as an internationally famous pianist, the narrator and his friend Wertheimer are 'losers'. They have not succeeded, and are obscure provincials. But over the course of the book, the narrator's desperate need to present his friend as a loser, to exempt himself from that dread category, and ultimately his distasteful tendency to see Wertheimer's suicide as the ultimate mark of his loserdom, become highly suspect. We slowly see that the narrator may not be entirely sane, that he has a kind of murderous envy of Gould, a competitive rivalry with Wertheimer and a deep guilt over Wertheimer's suicide. And that he is in love with both Gould and Wertheimer. Of all this he seems largely unaware. The reader is privy to the narrator's fantasy, a fantasy more enraged and systematic than that of Chekhov's officer perhaps, but different in degree, not in kind.

III

What do writers do when they seriously notice the world? Perhaps they do nothing less than rescue the life of things from their death – from two deaths, one small and one large: from the 'death' which literary form always threatens to impose on life, and from actual death. Which is to say, they rescue us from our death. I mean the fading reality that besets details as they recede from us – the memories of our childhood, the almost-forgotten pungency of flavours, smells, textures: the slow death that we deal to the world by the sleep of our attention. Growing older, says Knausgaard, is like standing in front of a mirror while holding another behind one's head, and seeing the receding dance of images – 'becoming smaller and smaller as far as the eye could see'. Knausgaard's world is one in which the adventure of the ordinary – the inexhaustibility of the ordinary as a child once experienced it ('the taste of salt that could fill your summer days to saturation') – is steadily retreating; in which things and objects and sensations are pacing towards meaninglessness. In such a world, the writer's task is to rescue the adventure from this slow retreat: to bring meaning, colour, and life back to the most ordinary things – to soccer boots and grass, to cranes and trees and airports, and even to Gibson guitars and Roland amplifiers and Old Spice and Ajax. 'You could still buy Slazenger tennis rackets, Tretorn balls, and Rossignol skis, Tyroka bindings and Koflack boots,' he writes. 'The houses where we lived were still standing, all of them. The sole difference, which is the difference between a child's reality and an adult's, was that they were no longer laden with meaning. A pair of Le Coque soccer boots was just a pair of football boots. If I felt anything when I held a pair in my hands now it was only a hangover from my childhood, nothing else, nothing in itself. The same with the sea, the same with the rocks, the same with the taste of salt that could fill your summer days to saturation, now it was just salt, end of story. The world was the same, yet it wasn't, for its meaning had been displaced, and was still being displaced, approaching closer and closer to meaninglessness.'

Literature, like art, pushes against time's fancy – makes us insomniacs in the halls of habit, offers to rescue the life of things from the dead. A story is told about the artist Oskar Kokoschka, who was leading a live drawing class. The students were bored and doing dull work, so

Kokoschka whispered to the model and told him to collapse to the ground. Kokoschka went over to the prone body, listened to his heart, pronounced him dead. The class was deeply shocked. Then the model stood up, and Kokoschka said: 'Now draw him as though you were aware he was alive and not dead!' What might that painting, in fiction, of a live body, look like? It would paint a body that was truly alive, but in such a way that we might be able to see that a body is always really dying; it would understand that life is shadowed by mortality, and thus make a death-seeing metaphysics of Kokoschka's life-giving aesthetics. (Isn't this what makes serious noticing truly *serious*?) It might read like this passage from a late story by Saul Bellow, 'Something to Remember Me By'. It is a paragraph about a drunken Irishman, McKern, who has passed out on a couch: 'I looked in at McKern, who had thrown down the coat and taken off his drawers. The parboiled face, the short nose pointed sharply, the life signs in the throat, the broken look of his neck, the black hair of his belly, the short cylinder between his legs ending in a spiral of loose skin, the white shine of the shins, the tragic expression of his feet.' This is perhaps what Kokoschka had in mind: Bellow is painting, in words, a model, who might or might not be alive: a painting that threatens at any moment to become a still life. So his character looks very hard at McKern, the way an anxious young parent does at a sleeping baby, to check that it is still alive. And he is still alive – just: *the life signs in the throat.*

Although Nabokov was too competitive to say anything decent about his peer Saul Bellow, it is hard to read this description of a man asleep without thinking of Nabokov's words, in one of his lectures, on how the great writer 'models a man asleep':

> To minor authors is left the ornamentation of the commonplace: these do not bother about any re-inventing of the world; they merely try to squeeze the best they can out of a given order of things, out of traditional patterns of fiction . . . But the real writer, the fellow who sends planets spinning and models a man asleep and eagerly tampers with the sleeper's rib, that kind of author has no given values at his disposal: he must create them himself. The art of writing is a very futile business if it does not imply first of all the art of seeing the world as the potentiality of fiction.

Nabokov's is a highly self-serving and romantic view of the author, who seems to have no indebtedness to any other author; indeed, in Nabokov's mythology, this writer, who fashions humans from ribs, is God Himself, which might well mean Vladimir Vladimirovich Nabokov.

But Kokoschka and Nabokov have hold of a central truth. Surely it is no surprise that we so often remember details that concern the deaths of real people ('famous last words', and so on) and fictional characters. Isn't this because at such moments writers are snatching the details of life, and the life of details, from the extinction that surrounds and threatens them? Montaigne, in his essay 'Of Cruelty', writes about the last minutes of Socrates's life, and how he is said to have scratched his leg. 'By that quiver of pleasure that he feels in scratching his leg after the irons were off, does he not betray a like sweetness and joy in his soul at being unfettered by past discomforts and prepared to enter into the knowledge of things to come?' But whereas Montaigne is essentially pre-novelistic, because he has a tendency to moralise about such details, and sees this moment as an example not of accident but of forthright moral vigour, a later writer like Tolstoy sees such a gesture as accidental or automatic – as life just instinctively desiring to extend itself beyond death. I am thinking of the moment witnessed by Pierre in *War and Peace*, when he sees a young Russian, blindfolded and about to be executed by firing squad, fiddle with his blindfold, perhaps in order to make it a little more comfortable.

This is the life-surplus, pushing itself beyond death, outliving death. Think of Tolstoy's Ivan Ilyich. As he nears his death, at the moment of greatest loneliness, he remembers the plums of his childhood, and the way that when you got down to the pit of the fruit, *the saliva would flow*. When Bellow's character Moses Herzog sees lobsters behind the glass of a Manhattan fishmonger, he sees their 'feelers bent', pressed up against the glass – the complaint of life against its deathly imprisonment. When the contemporary American novelist Rachel Kushner sees a squashed cockroach on a New York pavement, she sees its long wispy antennae 'swiping around for signs of its own life'. In Lydia Davis's story 'Grammar Questions', the narrator comes to the conclusion that her dying father is pure negation, has become nothing more than the adverb 'not' (hence the story's title) – and yet what she remembers, what *extends out* of her story, is the way her father is frowning as he lies in his sickbed, as if irritated. She has seen this frown many times in her life: it is what Bellow would call a 'life sign'.

To notice is to rescue, to redeem; to save life from itself. One of the characters in Marilynne Robinson's novel *Housekeeping* is described as a girl who 'felt the life of perished things'. In the same book, Robinson writes of how Jesus raised Lazarus from the dead, and even restored the severed ear of the soldier who came to rescue him, 'a fact that allows us to hope the resurrection will reflect a considerable attention to detail'. I like the idea that heaven might reward us for what we have lost by paying attention to detail, that heaven must perforce be a place of serious noticing. But perhaps we can bring back life, or extend life, here on earth, by doing the same: by applying what Walter Benjamin once called 'the natural prayer of the soul: attentiveness'. We can bring the dead back by applying the same attentiveness to their shades as we apply to the world around us – by looking harder: by transfiguring the object.

Benjamin's phrase comes in a letter to Adorno about Kafka; and perhaps Adorno was recalling this idea of attentiveness when he wrote, in *Negative Dialectics*, that 'if the thought really yielded to the object, if its attention were on the object, not on its category, the very objects would start talking under the lingering eye'.

See, there they are, talking to us: the poplar, the lilac and the roses. That peppermint tingle. The kiss.

3

USING EVERYTHING

I

THE BOOK THAT HAD the profoundest effect on me, when I was growing up, was not a novel or a book of poems; was not the Bible or Shakespeare's *Collected Works*, or *The Hobbit* or *Dune*, or any of the high or low stories that are canonically invoked when readers and writers look back in fondness. It was a book called *Novels and Novelists: A Guide to the World of Fiction*, edited by the wayward (and perhaps slightly insane) poet and man of letters, Martin Seymour-Smith. I found it in 1981, when I was fifteen, at Waterloo Station, on a table piled with discounted books. Utilitarian, pragmatic, bound in hideous butterscotch-coloured covers, fatally lacking in prestige, it looked as if it had been born in a permanently remaindered state, like a movie going straight to video. It promised sections on the Origins and Development of the Novel, on Crime Fiction and Science Fiction, on the Novel and Cinema and, most usefully, a section entitled 'Novelists: An Alphabetical

Guide'. On the front jacket there were nine photographs and engravings of writers, four of whom I could identify: John Fowles, Virginia Woolf (the flattering profile shot that people pinned above their desks), Leo Tolstoy, Henry James, Charles Dickens, Mark Twain, Saul Bellow, John Le Carré and Alison Lurie. An odd group, indicative of the book's ramshackle hospitality.

A chapter on 'The Novelist at Work' had alluring photographs of Nabokov wearing one of those Russian hats that look like a furry bird's nest, Hemingway, shirtless and tanned, typing in his bedroom in Cuba, Beryl Bainbridge 'at the small work table in her home in north London', and Len Deighton, sitting 'in his cluttered, but comfortable study', apparently warming himself by the fire. I took a good look at Deighton's room, and noticed with satisfaction that its tall window seemed to have been hung with a large sheet of clear plastic, a trick I knew well from my childhood of draughty studies in northern English vicarages. It was basic insulation, but, comically, never seemed to work very well. And as the sub-aqueous light came milkily through its plastic filter, so the chilly, ill-favoured room would take on the quality of a book-lined submarine. Of Deighton's work methods, the book informs us:

With a totally non-literary working-class background, he began his first book, *The Ipcress File* (1962), without any idea even of how long a novel was . . .

Soon, however, he developed an extremely professional way of life, drawing up elaborate preliminary work-sheets for each character, often including a random newspaper picture to indicate general appearance . . . He is quick to take advantage of every advance in typewriter technology.

And when he was not breathlessly keeping up with type-writer technology, Deighton was apparently living in nice pre-modern isolation, the archetype of the lucky bastard nailed by Philip Larkin as 'the shit in his shuttered chateau':

He now lives in Ireland, with a house in Portugal, and the isolation is very necessary to him, freeing him from distractions; he achieved this in London by living in the East End and having all his telephone calls either routed via a message agency or sent by teleprinter. In Ireland, he lives without television, having calculated that the evenings thus freed give him an extra day to work in.

I have never forgotten the following information, from the same chapter, about Emile Zola's work habits: 'He claimed that at times the effort of struggling with a rebel-lious passage actually caused him to have an erection.'

But it was the alphabetical gazetteer of novelists and short-story writers that really drew me. It was as exciting as looking at maps of the Scottish Highlands (Spean Bridge to Skye), or glossy car magazines, or a timetable for the Zurich-to-Milan night train. Each of the 1,348 authors was given a brief summary, ranging in size from forty to 250 words. These introductions were often opinionated, always evaluative, generally shrewd, sometimes amusingly wrong-headed. The range was dazzling, an undiscovered country full of hazy place-names: from Sylvia Ashton Warner (a New Zealander) to Sylvia Townsend Warner (English) and everyone in between: Alphonse Daudet, Osamu Dazai, Philip K. Dick, Vicki Baum, William Gass ('He is difficult to read, but certain passages in his fiction are lively and revelatory'); Witold Gombrowicz (the entry for whom runs, in its entirety: 'Polish novelist, dramatist and story-writer: one of the great experimentalists of the century, who suggested to his puzzled readers that they should "dance with" his books rather than analyse them. This is good advice. *Ferdydurke* is his most interesting novel'); A.S. Byatt ('She has puzzled readers, but has much to say'); Italo Svevo, Fritz Leiber, Geoffrey Household, Manzoni, Fontane, Melville, Zane Grey, Grace Metalious (author of *Peyton Place*); Dick Francis. There was an American historical novelist mysteriously named Winston Churchill (1871–1947): 'His methods and interpretations were superficial, but he was highly professional.' Along with Edmund Wilson, Angus Wilson, Colin Wilson, Ethel Wilson and Sloan Wilson (author of *The Man in the Grey Flannel Suit*).

Who *were* all these people? The summaries were quirky, but given the form and limits of the book, often accurate and intelligent. Apparently anything could be said, and there was an old-fashioned, sometimes dubious, shrewd and gossipy recourse to biography. Decades later, I am still struck by how much this book got right:

> Lawrence was not a good thinker, and to the extent that his elaboration of these doctrines – his increasingly neurotic concern with them – interferes with his art, he is a failure: his ideas become more and more confused, and he lacked self-criticism. Yet his art springs from his celebration of human instinct, and when he is studying behaviour in the light of his intuition he is an exquisite and beautiful writer.

It is not radical or great criticism, it wouldn't withstand scrutiny as academic analysis, but it rides a steady popular median quite well. Sometimes, as with the great nineteenth-century Prussian novelist Theodor Fontane, whom I wouldn't read until I was in my late thirties, there was an inspiring gesture of aesthetic advocacy: 'His achievement has not been fully appreciated in English-speaking countries, although the translation of *Effi Briest* in 1967 has begun to bring him the readers he deserves.' On Iris Murdoch: 'She has since published a book a year each compromised by faults which only lurked in her earlier fiction: an unreal, febrile, over-charged brilliance;

concentration on plot at the expense of developing characters; a *faiblesse* for arch donnish gags.' (At fifteen, I didn't know what a *faiblesse* was, and barely knew what an arch donnish gag was, but I liked the sound of both.)

The book had a daunting and, to the teenage aspirant, deeply enthralling obsession with 'greatness'. A reigning assumption of *Novels and Novelists* was that writers must aim for greatness, and that minor books are books that have missed greatness. It was like being caught in the relentless world of Thomas Bernhard, minus the suicide. Looking at my old copy, I see that I have solemnly underlined the following words, from the entry on Kafka: 'By the end of World War II he was established as one of the century's greatest writers – probably the greatest.' On Proust: 'There is undoubtedly a snob cult of Proust, but he is nonetheless a very great writer.' I was deeply impressed by the description of Pavese's novel *The Moon and the Bonfires* – not that I had read it, of course (I would not read this beautiful novel until my late twenties, and then as a direct consequence of Seymour-Smith's enthusiasm for it) – and made sure to underline the following vigorously intimidating words: 'His last novel *The Moon and the Bonfires* examines the whole of Italian life at three levels; it has not been surpassed technically in this century, and is unlikely to be.' *And is unlikely to be.* V.S. Naipaul, whom, thank goodness, I *had* actually read, was presented as 'one of the six or seven major English-language novelists of his generation'.

(That pseudo-exact 'six or seven' – was Naipaul the first or the seventh of that elastic little elite?)

To up the evaluative ante, at the end of each summary two or three of the author's books were selected and rated, according to Readability, Plot, Characterisation and Literary Quality (RPCL). In each category five stars was tops, and one star was bottom. It was literary Siskel and Ebert. *The Portrait of a Lady*, a novel I was studying in school and greatly admired, got five stars in all four categories, and I appended a pompous tick, along with a scribbled 'I agree'. Books that got the prized twenty stars were rare, and were obviously 'very great' – Proust, Musil's *Young Törless*, *Middlemarch*, *Under the Volcano*, Chekhov's Collected Tales, *The Man Who Loved Children*, Hamsun's *Mysteries*, Pirandello's stories (and how right *Novels and Novelists* was about *that* writer's lovely stories, I would discover, much later in life). I used the alphabetical list as a train-spotter used his book of locomotive numbers: a single cross next to an author meant that I had read him or her. (Dismayingly few of these.) Two crosses meant 'author of high importance, but not yet read'. Three crosses meant 'author of some importance, but not yet read'. Wyndham Lewis, an author I have still never really read, got two; George Sand (likewise, alas) got three. Two next to Claude Simon ('He is perhaps the most analytic novelist alive'), four for Delmore Schwartz. And so on.

It is easy to mock a book like this – the blunt earnestness, the aesthetic tyranny, the voracious and somehow rather male obsession with ratings and numbers and grades and total encyclopaedic coverage. But I am struck now, as I doubtless was then in a different way, by its sweet, radical innocence. These short descriptions seemed like passionate messages sent to me from inside the world of literature: they had an intoxicating air of urgent aesthetic advocacy, an apparent proximity to the creative source, a deep certainty that writing mattered, that great books were worth living and dying for, that, consequently, bad or boring books needed to be identified and winnowed out. This, I felt, was how writers spoke about literature! And the book also incarnated an important doubleness – even if, at that age, I could not quite have identified it. On the one hand, Seymour-Smith seemed to care very much about evaluation, about sorting out the merely okay, the good, the very good and the 'great'. On the other hand, the book's crazily comprehensive hospitality seemed to undermine that project; or, if not quite to undermine it, then to remind the reader that aesthetic hierarchies are fluid, personal, eccentric, always subject to revision and quite possibly a bit incoherent. It seemed that literary evaluation – deciding whether you like a work, how good or bad it is and why – could not be separated from the general messiness of being alive. You might love Chekhov, but you might also love Len Deighton, yet in a quite different way from loving Chekhov, and your love of Chekhov might be slightly influenced by the trivial knowledge that he named one of his dachshunds Quinine . . .

Wordsworth called his brother John 'the silent poet', and in this sense, perhaps, we are all silent poets. But really we are all silent critics, since not everyone has a poetic eye but everyone has an opinionated tongue. To evaluate is not only natural and instinctive, it is what writers supremely do, so that when we are evaluative we are writerly. It used to be the case, twenty or thirty years ago, that the very thing that most matters to writers, the first question they ask of a literary work – *is it any good?* – was often largely irrelevant to university teachers. Writers are naturally interested in what you could call aesthetic success: in order to create something successful one must learn about other people's successful and not-so-successful creations. To the academy, much of this value-chat resembled, and sometimes still does resemble, mere impressionism. Literary theory was by no means the only reason that the academy grew steadily more wary of evaluation. True, some postmodern and deconstructive thought is suspicious of the artwork's claim to coherence, and can be consequently indifferent or hostile to the discussion of its formal success. But conventional, non-theoretical criticism and scholarship often acted as if questions of value were irrelevant, or canonically settled. To spend one's time explaining how a text works was not necessarily ever to talk about how well it works, though it might seem that the latter is implicit in the former. Who bothers, while teaching *The Portrait of a Lady* for the nth time, to explain to students that it's a beautiful book? But for most writers, greedy to learn and emulate,

71

this is the only important question. Times have changed, and what were once called the theory wars have ended in a productive stalemate, in which, roughly speaking, both sides won – cherished canonical works were not violently displaced in the end, while the canon was indeed fruitfully expanded; and all literary critics, even the more traditional ones, learned crucial, transformative insights from deconstruction and post-structuralism.

But it is still worth trying to identify and practise something one might call *writer's criticism*, and to distinguish it somewhat from more academic traditions. Academic literary criticism, after all, is a belated institutional usurper. Before the last decades of the nineteenth century, the study of literary texts was confined to the study of religious or classical literature. It is not until around the First World War that the formal study of modern English literature begins to take its modern shape, partly as a weapon in the arsenal of Germanophobic English nationalism. The rise of what would be called English Studies starts at this time with the appointment of professors enjoined to practise them. Many of these professors, as has been gleefully pointed out, were rank amateurs. The triply named bookman – Sir Arthur Quiller-Couch, Arthur Clutton Brock – gave a few connoisseurial lectures and retired to his club, to doze amid a cloudy consensus. It was a world in which, say, G.S. Gordon, when he succeeded Walter Raleigh as Merton Professor of English at Oxford, was said to have got the job largely on the strength of his contributions to the *Times Literary Supplement*. Many of these early professors gave evaluation its bad reputation, and are responsible for the powerful rebellion against evaluation, and the reaching for quasi-scientific status, that have characterised most movements in literary criticism since the New Criticism of the 1940s and '50s.

But of course literary criticism had existed long before Oxford, Cambridge, Edinburgh, Aberdeen, Paris, Yale and Harvard took it up. It existed *as literature*, and belonged to the literary tradition, and was practised by writers; and it is the kind of criticism that should give evaluation a good reputation. I mean Puttenham on rhetoric, Sidney on poetry, Samuel Johnson on everyone, Hazlitt's essays, Coleridge (a critic both theoretical and practical, who coined the term 'practical criticism'), Baudelaire on Goya, Virginia Woolf, Benjamin on Proust or Kafka, V.S. Pritchett on the Russian and English novel (neither Woolf nor Pritchett went to university), Randall Jarrell, Elizabeth Hardwick, Julien Gracq. This is the tradition of writerly criticism, the tradition of the writer-critic, which perseveres and continues. (Think of Joseph Brodsky's essays, of Czesław Miłosz on Dostoevsky, Milan Kundera on the European novel, Zadie Smith, Ali Smith, David Foster Wallace on contemporary writing, and so on.)

Such criticism, like *Novels and Novelists*, is situated in the world, not behind scholarly walls, and is unafraid of making use of anything that comes to mind or hand. Criticism, after all, is supremely pragmatic. Mark Greif, a founder of the New York-based literary journal *n+1*, recently quoted Kenneth Burke (himself a non-attached free-floating American intellectual, who dropped out of Columbia to write) on the proper basis for criticism: 'The main ideal of criticism, as I conceive it, is to use all there is to use.' Greif continues, wisely: 'This precedes Burke as many great critics' method, and it will outlast those of us doing our short span of work now.'

II

There is a famous essay by Thomas De Quincey, called 'On the Knocking at the Gate in *Macbeth*'. De Quincey tries to explain, to his own satisfaction, why he is so affected by the scene in Act 2 of *Macbeth* when, after the murder of the king, a knocking on the gate is heard. The porter arrives, tells us about the ups and downs of heavy drinking ('it provokes the desire, but it takes away the performance') and slowly opens the door: Macduff and Lennox have arrived, and are looking for the king. De Quincey recognises that something strange occurs at this moment, some peculiar shift, but can't work out why. The problem, he decides, is that he was trying to use his 'understanding' – and yet, he reminds us, the understanding is not helpful but actually obstructs proper analysis: 'The mere understanding, however useful and indispensable, is the meanest faculty in the human mind and the most to be distrusted: and yet the great majority of people trust to nothing else.' His example: ask someone to draw a street, anyone who is not previously prepared for the demand by a knowledge of perspective. That person will allow his understanding to overrule his eyes. He will draw a horizontal line, because that is what he thinks he should do, and will fail to produce the desired pictorial effect.

De Quincey continues that his 'understanding' could furnish him with no reason why the knocking at the gate should have any special effect. In fact, 'my understanding said positively that it could *not* produce any effect. But I knew better: I felt that it did: and I waited and clung to the problem until further knowledge should enable me to solve it.'

Soon enough, further knowledge comes along, in the form of the Ratcliff Highway murders, which took place in London's East End, in December 1811. After the first of these murders, an incident similar to the Shakespearean motif apparently occurred: a knocking was heard at the door, soon after 'the work of extermination was complete'. Shakespeare thus proposed an invention that became a reality. Eventually, De Quincey announces, 'I solved it to my satisfaction.' But like a good essayist he takes his time withholding exactly what that solution is. When we see someone faint, says De Quincey, the most affecting moment is when the person comes round, and this announces 'the recommencement of suspended life'. Or one might be walking in a great city like London on the day of some great national funeral, when the streets are empty and stilled. And then the return to life, after the funeral is over, suddenly reminds us of the earlier suspension of ordinary business. 'All action in any direction is best expounded, measured, and made apprehensible by reaction.' Now apply this to *Macbeth*. De Quincey concludes that in order for us to appreciate the play we have to feel sympathy for the murderer; we enter into his feelings and are made to understand them. When Macbeth and his wife do their dreadful deeds, ordinary, healthy life ceases, but we were not aware of that suspension because we were spending our time in Macbeth's mind, through his soliloquies. The knocking is what he calls 'the pulse of life beginning to beat again': 'and the re-establishment of the goings-on of the world in which we live, first make us profoundly sensible of the awful parenthesis that had suspended them'.

It is a wonderfully intelligent essay. The most obvious effect of the knocking and the porter's rowdy comedy – its jarring difference from the preceding horror – doesn't much interest De Quincey; he assumes that. But the *next* most obvious effect, that the knocking is simply the pulse of life returning, doesn't interest him that much, either – except insofar as the return of ordinary life reminds us of a previous lack: reminds us *that a suspension of life occurred of which we had not been previously aware.* Thus the essay's conclusion to its own riddle is embodied in its form: just as De Quincey discovers that the knocking reminds us of something we had neglected (the suspension of ordinary life), so his essay stumbles upon a suspension that *he* had neglected: the suspension of his intuitive intelligence, its death at the hands of what he calls (puzzlingly to us moderns) 'the understanding'. He had to allow his intuition to come back to life.

I like, too, that he makes a connection, not between the knocking at the door and the knocking of Macbeth's murderous heart (again, the obvious figurative connection, encouraged by Shakespeare), but with the pulse of ordinary life itself. And there is something fine in the Burkean way (Kenneth, not Edmund) that this essay 'uses all there is to use'. De Quincey has an interpretative problem to solve, and he treats this not like the hermetic hermeneut, canted over his well-thumbed text, but like the urban stroller who wrote *Confessions of an English Opium-Eater*: he thinks about a real murder in London, he reaches for the memory of wandering the city streets during the suspension of ordinary activity. An aesthetic problem is solved, in part, by . . . living. By ordinary existence. Because he uses all there is to use, he is naturally democratic.

De Quincey is not afraid of simplicity, and is not afraid to admit incomprehension. The two may be related. Often, simplicity is the only possible way of saying of a novel or a poem, 'this moved me', 'this was beautiful', 'this *silences* me'. This confounds me. Simplicity is the climate of the preliminary, the wide realm in which we utter our first affective responses. De Quincey goes from simplicity to complexity, but his complexity is fairly simple. Criticism by uncommon writers often has a way of saying, and seeing, the simple large things. When the great short-story writer Eudora Welty, for instance, writes of symbols in fiction, and says that one way of thinking about Moby-Dick is that he was so large a symbol that he just *had* to be a whale, she is squeezing into a piece of novelistic wit a deep and simple point about how fiction uses symbols.

A lot of the criticism I most admire is not especially analytical but is really a kind of passionate re-description. Sometimes it's a kind of critical act to hear a poet or novelist read aloud her poem or piece of his prose. There is a good reason, after all, why writers have always been interested in actors and acting; there is a sense in which the actor is the purest, the first critic. The written equivalent of the reading-aloud of a poem or a play is the retelling of the literature one is talking about; the good critic has an awareness that criticism means, in part, telling a story about the story you are reading, as De Quincey binds us into the story of his readerly detection.

I would call this kind of critical retelling a way of writing *through* books, not just about them. This writing-through is often achieved by using the language of metaphor and simile that literature itself uses. It is a recognition that literary criticism is unique because one has the great privilege of performing it in the same medium one is describing. (Pity the poor music critic, the forlorn art critic!)

When Coleridge writes of Swift that 'he had the soul of Rabelais but dwelling in a dry place', or when Henry James says that Balzac was so devoted to his work that he became a kind of 'Benedictine of the actual' (a phrase he liked so much that he plagiarised his own earlier essay on Flaubert); when Pritchett laments that Ford Madox Ford never fell into that 'determined stupor' out of which great artistic work comes – these writers are producing images that are qualitatively indistinguishable from the metaphors and similes in their so-called 'creative' work. They are speaking to literature in its own language. This speaking to literature in its own language is indeed the equivalent of a musical or theatrical performance; an act of critique which is at the same time a re-voicing. There may also be an element of writerly rivalry or proximity, the writer displaying her own talent to the subject. Virginia Woolf's essays are the great example here, because when she wrote for the *TLS* all contributions were anonymous: her journalism had to sign itself by style. Everyone knew when a piece was by Woolf.

Metaphor is the language of literature, and hence of literary criticism. The philosopher Ted Cohen, in his book *Thinking of Others: On the Talent for Metaphor*, makes a persuasive case that metaphor is central to the ways in which we read fiction and to the ways in which we identify with other characters, put ourselves in their shoes. Cohen starts with the simple, sometimes overlooked fact that metaphor is akin to an imaginative identification. When we say, metaphorically, that 'A is B', we are induced to think of A *as* B, and this leads to new thoughts about A. Cohen says this ability to 'see' A as B is a crucial human gift; he calls it having a 'talent for metaphor'. This is not just a poetic talent for making metaphor (for seeing the root of a tree as resembling a paw, as Sartre did, or a taxi meter like a moral owl, as Bishop did). He thinks it is the engine driving how we identify with characters in novels, because metaphor asks us 'to think of one thing as something it is plainly not' – what he calls metaphors of 'personal identification'.

Cohen essentially argues that for me to assert, say, 'I am Barack Obama' or 'I am Macbeth' is a kind of sympathetic identification that belongs in the family of metaphor. He concedes that most people wouldn't consider 'I am Barack Obama' to be a metaphor in the same way that 'Juliet is the sun' is a metaphor. Still, says Cohen, the knack for grasping these sentences is the same as the knack for grasping metaphors, and when we read about fictional characters a metaphorical transaction is going on. This is because our identification with fictional characters is not a matter of strict identity, but of figurative identification. When we say that A can be seen as B, we don't posit that A and B share the same properties, but we suggest that 'B has some property that A can be thought of as having, when in fact the property is not literally a property of A'.

In other words, to return to an earlier phrase, *fiction is the game of not quite*. That is what we find De Quincey arguing in his essay – he is keen to point out that we missed the suspension of ordinary life because we had been identifying with the murderer. But not literally: Shakespeare must 'throw the interest on the murderer: our sympathy must be with *him* (of course I mean a sympathy of comprehension by which we enter into his feelings, and are made to understand them – not a sympathy of pity or approbation).' And then De Quincey enacts his own leap of sympathy, whereby in order to fathom the effect of that knocking, he must experience for himself what that suspension and reawakening of life felt like. Coleridge famously talked of succumbing to the mimesis of the fictional work as a suspension of disbelief; through the suspension of disbelief De Quincey manages the suspension of his 'understanding', and thus reaches the answer to his question.

Ted Cohen quotes from a paper written in 1949, called 'Critical Communication', by the philosopher Arnold Isenberg. In what Cohen calls 'an astonishingly brief and effective argument', Isenberg undermines the common notion that by citing the artwork's property the critic is producing a *reason* in support of value judgement. What the critic must hope to do, said Isenberg, is, by drawing attention to properties of the artwork, induce in his audience a *similar view* of the work. This way, in Isenberg's phrase, he might achieve a 'sameness of vision' in his audience (that is, a sameness of vision, an identity, of audience and critic). Cohen goes on to point out that this is a brilliant description of the use of metaphor: 'When your metaphor is "X is Y" you are hoping that I will see X as you do, namely as Y, and, most likely, although your proximate aim is to get me to see X in this way, your ultimate wish is that I will feel about X as you do.'

In summary: metaphor is a form of identification; to identify with a fictional character is a kind of identification, and thus a metaphorical leap; and criticism seems to act in a similar way, by enacting a sameness or likeness of vision, an act of figurative identification, whereby the critic says, in effect, 'I will work to enable you to see the text as I do.'

The only thing to add is that if this 'sameness of vision' is effectively metaphorical, then a language of metaphor – the writer-critic's own metaphoricity – is the embodied language of that process, the best available enactment of it. Second, if imaginative identification is at bottom metaphorical, then the reader's (or critic's) metaphorical identification is very close to the writer's. As Shakespeare must imagine himself into the role of Macbeth, so the reader must do so, too, and is thus partaking of the creative act. The readerly act is also the writerly act. And if the critic's writing-up of that identification is also metaphorical, then we can bestow a slightly enriched meaning on Arnold Isenberg's original phrase 'sameness of vision'. We are all, writer, reader and rewriter (the critic), engaged in a sameness of vision which is in some ways a *sameness of writing*.

Here are two examples of sameness of vision, sameness of writing. The first is from Virginia Woolf's

82

biography of the art critic and curator Roger Fry; the other from my own experience. Both are scenes of critical performance, in a theatre-space. Woolf describes hearing Fry give a public lecture in London – a stiff, formal affair, with the critic in evening dress and holding a long pointer:

All that he had done again and again in his books. But here there was a difference. As the next slide slid over the sheet there was a pause. He gazed afresh at the picture. And then in a flash he found the word he wanted; he added on the spur of the moment what he had just seen as if for the first time. That, perhaps, was the secret of his hold over his audience. They could see the sensation strike and form; he could lay bare the very moment of perception. So with pauses and spurts the world of spiritual reality emerged in slide after slide – in Poussin, in Chardin, in Rembrandt, in Cézanne – in its uplands and its lowlands, all connected, all somehow made whole and entire, upon the great screen in the Queen's Hall. And finally the lecturer, after looking long through his spectacles, came to a pause. He was pointing to a late work by Cézanne, and he was baffled. He shook his head; his stick rested on the floor. It went, he said, far beyond any analysis of which he was capable. And so instead of saying, 'Next slide,' he bowed, and the audience emptied itself into Langham Place.

For two hours they had been looking at pictures. But they had seen one of which the lecturer himself was unconscious – the outline of the man against the screen, an ascetic figure in evening dress who paused and pondered, and then raised his stick and pointed. That was a picture that would remain in memory together with the rest, a rough sketch that would serve many of the audience in years to come as the portrait of a great critic, a man of profound sensibility but of exacting honesty, who, when reason could penetrate no further, broke off; but was convinced, and convinced others, that what he saw was there.

It is all here, in this beautiful passage: criticism as passionate creation ('as if for the first time'); criticism as modesty, as the mind putting the 'understanding' into abeyance ('he was baffled'); criticism as simplicity and near-silence ('It went, he said, far beyond any analysis of which he was capable'); criticism as sameness of vision ('was convinced, and convinced others, that what he saw was there'). Fry 'found the word he wanted', but Woolf, using narrative much as she does in *To the Lighthouse*, withholds from us what that word was; slowly, gradually, 'found the word he wanted' cedes to wordless humility and the fierce conviction that 'what he saw was there': a movement whereby, through a process akin to mimetic desire, the audience began to experience what Fry saw, experienced with him a sameness of vision.

A few years ago, I was in Edinburgh, and went with my father to hear the pianist Alfred Brendel give an illustrated talk about Beethoven's piano sonatas. We were late, and arrived at the hall breathless and sweaty. But all was serene inside. Brendel sat at a table, with a concert grand piano behind him. He talked – or mumbled, rather – from his lecture notes, peering down at his text through thick spectacles. He has a strong Austrian accent, unaffected by decades of living in England. Every so often he would turn to the piano to play a few bars, as illustration. But something remarkable occurred when he quoted: even to play a short phrase, he became not a quoter but a performer, not merely a critic but an artist-critic: physically, he had to enter the trance-like state in which he performs whole concerts (his customary shudderings, phantom mastication, closed eyes, swooning and tilting). He could not *blandly* quote the music, in the way that one might read a line from French without bothering to put on the 'proper' French accent. He had to become, as it were, properly French. In this sense, *he could not quote*. He could only re-create; which is to say, he could only create. It was intensely frustrating to hear, again and again, three bars of the most beautiful Beethoven, perfectly performed, only to have them break off and be replaced by the pianist's inaudible Viennese mumbling. Play on, play on, don't talk! I soundlessly urged. The mumbling quickly became of no interest or importance; one lived for the next pianistic performance, one was swinging from beauty to beauty, high above the dun currents of the prosaic. His 'quotes' overwhelmed his commentary; he was approaching Walter Benjamin's idea of a book entirely made of quotations.

Perhaps the analogy with literary criticism is imperfect, because the literary critic lacks this precise ability to inflect his chosen quotes as the musician performs his. But let Brendel's wordy mumbling stand for a kind of literary criticism condemned to exteriority, a writing-about rather than a writing-through the text, a flat commentary, banished from the heart of the creative. And let Brendel's performance on the piano, his inability to quote without also creating, stand for the kind of criticism that is a writing through a text, the kind of criticism that is at once critique and re-description.

4

SECULAR HOMELESSNESS

I

I HAD A PIANO teacher who used to talk about the most familiar musical cadence – in which a piece returns, after wandering and variation, to its original key, the tonic – as 'going home'. It seemed so easy when music did it: who wouldn't want to swat away those black accidentals and come back to sunny C major? These satisfying resolutions are sometimes called 'perfect cadences'; there is a lovely subspecies called the 'English cadence', used often by composers like Tallis and Byrd, in which, just before the expected resolution, a dissonance sharpens its blade and seems about to wreck things – and is then persuaded home, as it should be.

I wish I could hear that English cadence again, the way I first properly heard it in Durham Cathedral. I was eleven years old. During the lesson, we choristers had been exchanging notes, probably sniggering at one of the more pompous priests – the one who, as he processed towards his stall, held his clasped hands pointing outwards from his breast, like a pious fish – and then we were up on our feet, and were singing 'O Nata Lux', by Thomas Tallis. I knew the piece but hadn't really listened to it. Now I was struck – assaulted, thrown – by its utter beauty: the soft equanimity of its articulation, like the voice of justice; the sweet dissonance, welcome as pain. That dissonance, with its distinctive Tudor sound, is partly produced by a movement known as 'false relation', in which the note you expect to hear in the harmony of a chord is shadowed by its nearest relation – the same note but a semitone off. As the Tallis was ending, I saw a middle-aged woman with a canvas shoulder-bag enter the shadowy hinterland at the back of the huge building. Standing so far away, a singular figure, she might have been a tentative tourist. But I knew the full bag, that coat I always wanted to be a bit more impressive than it was, the anxious rectitude of my mother's posture. She came every Tuesday afternoon, because the girls' school she taught at got out early then. My parents lived only a mile or so from the cathedral, but I had to board; Tuesday afternoons, before I went back to school, gave me the chance to exchange a few words, and grab whatever she brought in that bag – comics and sweets; and, more reliably, socks.

In my memory this is exactly what happened: the radiance of the music, the revelation of its beauty, the final cadences of the Tallis, and my happy glimpsing of my mother. But it happened thirty-seven years ago, and the scene has a convenient, dream-like composition. Perhaps I have really dreamed it. As I get older I dream more frequently of that magnificent cathedral – the long grey cool interior hanging somehow like memory itself. These are intense experiences, from which I awake hearing every single note of a piece of remembered music; happy dreams, never troubled. I like returning to that place in my sleep, even look forward to it.

But real life is a different matter. The few occasions I have returned to Durham have been strangely disappointing. My parents no longer live there; I no longer live in the country. The city has become a dream. Herodotus says that the Scythians were hard to defeat because they had no cities or settled forts: 'they carry their houses with them and shoot with bows from horseback . . . their dwellings are on their wagons. How can they fail to be invincible and inaccessible for others?' To have a home is to become vulnerable. Not just to the attacks of others, but to our own massacres of alienation: our campaigns of departure and return threaten to become mere adventures in voiding. I left my home twice – the first time, just after university, when I went to London, in the familiar march of the provincial for the metropolis. I borrowed a thousand pounds from the NatWest bank in Durham (an account I still have), rented a van one-way, put everything I owned into it and drove south; I remember thinking, as I waved at my parents and my sister, that the gesture was both authentic and oddly artificial, the authorised novelistic journey. In this way, many of us are homeless: the exodus of expansion. The second departure occurred in 1995, when at the age of thirty I left Britain for the United States. I was married to an American – to put it more precisely, I was married to an American citizen whose French father and Canadian mother, themselves immigrants, lived in the States. We had no children, and America would surely be new and exciting. We might even stay there for a few years – five at the most?

I have now lived eighteen years in the United States. It's feeble to say I didn't expect to stay as long; and ungrateful, or even meaningless or dishonest, to say I didn't want to. I must have wanted to; there has been plenty of gain. But I had so little concept of what might be lost. 'Losing a country', or 'losing a home', if I gave the matter much thought when I was young, was an acute world-historical event, forcibly meted out on the victim, lamented and canonised in literature and theory as 'exile' or 'displacement', and defined with appropriate termi-nality by Edward Said in his essay 'Reflections on Exile':

Exile is strangely compelling to think about but terrible to experience. It is the unhealable rift forced between a human being and a native place, between the self and its true home: its essential sadness can never be surmounted. And while it is true that literature and history contain heroic, romantic, glorious, even trium-phant episodes in an exile's life, these are no more than efforts meant to overcome the crippling sorrow of estrangement. The achievements of exile are permanently undermined by the loss of something left behind forever.

Said's emphasis on the self's 'true home' has a slightly theological, or perhaps Platonic, sound. When there is such universal homelessness, of both the forced and the unforced kind, the idea of a 'true home' surely suffers an amount of unsympathetic modification. Perhaps Said's implication is that unwanted homelessness only bears down on those who have a true home and thus always reinforces the purity of the origin, while voluntary homelessness – the softer emigration I am trying to define – means that home can't have been very 'true' after all. I doubt he intended that – but nonetheless, in the traditional reading, the desert of exile seems to need the oasis of primal belonging, the two held in a biblical clasp.

In that essay, Said distinguishes between exile, refugee, expatriate and émigré. Exile, as he understands it, is tragic homelessness, connected to the ancient punishment of banishment; he approves of Adorno's subtitle to *Minima Moralia*: *Reflections from a Mutilated Life*. It is hard to see how the milder, unforced journey I am describing could belong to this grander vision of suffering. 'Not going home' is not exactly the same as 'homelessness'. That nice old boarding-school standby, 'homesickness', might fit better, particularly if allowed a certain doubleness. I am sometimes homesick, where homesickness is a kind of longing for Britain and an irritation with Britain: sickness *for* and sickness *of*. I bump into plenty of people in America who tell me that they miss their native countries – Britain, Germany, Russia, Holland, South Africa – and who in the next breath say they cannot imagine returning. It is possible, I suppose, to miss home terribly, not know what home really is any more and refuse to go home, all at once. Such a tangle of feelings might then be a definition of luxurious freedom, as far removed from Said's tragic homelessness as can be imagined.

Logically, a refusal to go home should validate, negatively, the very idea of home, rather in the way that Said's idea of exile validates the idea of an original 'true home'. But perhaps the refusal to go home is consequent upon the loss, or lack, of home: as if those fortunate expatriates were really saying to me, 'I couldn't go back home because I wouldn't know how to any more.' And there is 'Home' and 'a home'. Authors used to be described on book dust-jackets as 'making a home': 'Mr Blackmur makes his home in Princeton, New Jersey.' I have made a home in the United States, but it is not quite Home. For instance, I have no strong desire to become an American citizen. Recently, when I arrived at Boston airport, the immigration officer commented on the length of time I've held a Green Card. 'A Green Card is usually considered a path to citizenship,' he said, a sentiment both irritatingly reproving and movingly patriotic. I mumbled something about how he was perfectly correct, and left it at that. But consider the fundamental openness and generosity of the gesture (along with the undeniable coercion): it's hard to imagine his British counterpart so freely offering citizenship – as if it were, indeed, uncomplicatedly *on offer*, a service or commodity. He was generously saying, 'Would you like to be an American citizen?' along with the less generous, 'Why don't you want to be an American citizen?' Can we imagine either sentiment being expressed at Heathrow airport? The poet and novelist Patrick McGuinness, in his book *Other People's Countries* (itself a rich analysis of home and homelessness; McGuiness is half-Irish and half-Belgian) quotes Simenon, who was asked why he didn't change his nationality, 'the way successful Francophone Belgians often did'. Simenon replied: 'There was no reason for me to be born Belgian, so there's no reason for me to stop being Belgian.' I wanted to say something similar, less wittily, to the immigration officer: precisely because I don't need to become an American citizen, to take it would seem flippant; leave its benefits for those who need a new land.

So whatever this state I am talking about is, this 'not going home', it is not tragic; there's probably something a bit ridiculous in these privileged laments – oh, sing 'dem Harvard blues, white boy! But I am trying to describe *some* kind of loss, some kind of falling away. (The gain is obvious enough and thus less interesting to analyse.) I asked Christopher Hitchens, long before he was terminally ill, where he would go if he had only a few weeks to live. Would he stay in America? 'No, I'd go to Dartmoor, without a doubt,' he told me. It was the landscape of his childhood. Dartmoor, not the MD Anderson Cancer Center in Houston. It's not uncommon for expatriates, émigrés, refugees and travellers to want to die 'at home'. The desire to return, after so long away, is gladly irrational, and is perhaps premised on the loss of the original home (as the refusal to go home may also be premised on the loss of home). Home swells as a sentiment because it has disappeared as an achievable reality. Marusya Tatarovich, the heroine of the novel *A Foreign Woman*, by the Russian émigré writer Sergei Dovlatov, comes to the conclusion that she has made a mistake in leaving Russia for New York City, and decides to return. Dovlatov, who left the Soviet Union for America in 1979, and who appears as himself in the novel, tries to talk her out of it. You've just forgotten what life is like there, he says: 'The rudeness, the lies.' She replies: 'If people are rude in Moscow, at least it's in Russian.' But she stays in America. I once saw, in Germany, a small exhibition of Samuel Beckett's correspondence to his German publisher. Many brief note-cards were arranged chronologically, the last written only a few months before his death. Beckett wrote to his publisher not in German but in French, a language in which he had of course made a home; but in the final year of his life, he switched to English. 'Going home,' I thought.

After so many years, life in America, or in my small part of America, has become my life. And life is made up of particulars: friends, conversation, dailiness of all sorts. I love, for instance, that certain New England states alert drivers that they are entering a built-up area with the sign 'Thickly Settled'. I love the Hudson River, its steady brown flow; generally, I like how most American rivers make their European rivals look like wan streams. There is the crimson livery of the Boar's Head trucks. Or the way the mailman, delivering the post in the dark winter afternoon, wears a little miner's lamp on his head, and peers down at his paper bundle. Large American radiators in old apartment buildings, with their hissing and ghostly clanking. A certain general store in New Hampshire that sells winter boots, hand cream, excellent bacon and firearms. I cherish the phrase 'Take it easy', and the scandalous idea that people would actually say this to each other! I am even fond, now, of things that reliably dumbfound the British – American sports, say; or the fact that the word *fortnight* does not exist; that *fudge* is just chocolate; and that seemingly no one can properly pronounce the words *croissant*, *milieu* or *bourgeois*.

But there is always the reality of a certain outsider-dom. Take the beautiful American train horn, the crushed klaxon peal you can hear almost anywhere in the States – at the end of my street at night-time, across a New Hampshire valley, in some small Midwestern town: a crumple of notes, blown out on an easy, loitering wail. It sounds less like a horn than a sudden prairie wind or an animal's cry.

That big easy loiter is, for me, the sound of America, whatever America is. But it must also be 'the sound of America' for thousands, perhaps millions, of non-Americans. It's a shared possession, not a personal one. I'm outside it; I appreciate it, as something slightly distant. It is unhistorical for me: it doesn't have my past in it, drags no old associations. (We lived about half a mile from the Durham station, and from my bedroom, at night I could hear the arrhythmic thunder of the big yellow-nosed Deltic diesels, as they pulled their shabby carriages onto the Victorian viaduct that curves out of town, bound for London or Edinburgh, and sometimes blew their parsimonious horns – the British Rail minor third.)

Or suppose I am looking down our Boston street, in dead summer. I see a familiar life: the clapboard houses, the porches, the heat-mirage hanging over the patched road (snakes of asphalt like black chewing-gum), the grey cement pavements (signed in one place, when the cement was new, by three young siblings), the heavy maple trees, the unkempt willow down at the end, an old white Cadillac with the bumper sticker 'Ted Kennedy has killed more people than my gun', and I feel . . . nothing: some recognition, but no comprehension, no real connection, no past, despite all the years I have lived there; just a tugging distance from it all. A panic suddenly overtakes me, and I wonder: how did I get here? And then the moment passes, and ordinary life closes itself around what had seemed, for a moment, a desperate lack.

Edward Said says that it is no surprise that exiles are often novelists, chess players, intellectuals. 'The exile's new world, logically enough, is unnatural, and its unreality resembles fiction.' He reminds us that Georg Lukács considered the novel the great form of what Lukács called 'transcendental homelessness'. I am certainly not an exile, but it is sometimes hard to shake the 'unreality' Said speaks of. I watch my children grow up as Americans in the same way that I might read about, or create, fictional characters. *They* are not fictional, of course, but their Americanism can sometimes seem unreal to me. 'I have an American seventh-grader,' I say to myself with amazement, as I watch my twelve-year-old daughter perform at one of those dastardly school events always held in gymnasiums. Doubtless, amazement attends all the stages of a child's growth – all is unexpected. But there is also that strange distance, the light veil of alienation thrown over everything.

And then there is the same light veil thrown over everything when I go back to Britain, too. When I was first living in the States, I was eager to keep up with life 'back at home' – who was in the Cabinet, the new music, what people were saying in the newspapers, how the schools were doing, the price of petrol, the shape of friends' lives. It became harder to do so, because the meaning of these things grew less and less personal. For me, English reality has disappeared into memory, has 'changed itself to past', as Larkin has it. I know very little about modern daily life in London, or Edinburgh, or Durham. There's a quality of masquerade when I return, as if I were putting on my wedding suit, to see if it still fits.

In America, I crave the English reality that has disappeared; childhood seems breathingly close. But the sense of masquerade persists: I gorge on nostalgia, on fondnesses that might have embarrassed me when I lived in Britain. Geoff Dyer writes funnily, in *Out of Sheer Rage*, about how, when he was living in Italy, he developed an obsession with reading the TV listings in English papers, even though he had never watched telly when he lived in England, and didn't like it. To hear a Geordie voice on an American news programme leaves me flushed with longing: the dance of that dialect, with its seasick Scandinavian pitch. And all those fabulous words: *segs* (the metal plates you'd bang onto your shoe-heels, to make sparks on the ground and act like a hard-nut); *kets* (sweets); *neb* (nose); *nowt* (nothing); *stotty-cake* (a kind of flat, doughy bread), *claggy* (sticky). The way northerners say *eee*, as an exclamation: 'Eee, it's red-hot today!' (Any temperature over about twenty degrees.) Recently, I heard the old song 'When the Boat Comes In' on National Public Radio, and almost wept.

Now come here, little Jacky
Now I've smoked me backy,
Let's have some cracky
Till the boat comes in

And you shall have a fishy
On a little dishy
You shall have a fishy
When the boat comes in.

But I really disliked that song when I was a boy. I never had a very northern accent. My father was born in London. It was important to my Scottish petty-bourgeois mother that I didn't sound like a Geordie. Friends used to say, with a bit of menace in their voices: 'You don't talk like a Durham lad. Where are you from?' Sometimes it was necessary to mimic the accent, to fit in, or to avoid getting beaten up. I could never say, as the man in the song 'Coming Home Newcastle' foolishly does: 'And I'm proud to be a Geordie / And to live in Geordie-land.'

My town was the university and the cathedral – it seemed that almost everyone who lived on our street was an academic (like my father) or a clergyman; and they didn't sound like Geordies. How vivid all those neighbours are, in my mind! And how strange they were. I think now that in the 1970s I caught the fading comet-end of allowable eccentricity. There was Mrs Jolley, though she was in fact anything but, who walked with three canes, one for the left leg and two (bound together with string) for the right. There was the dry, bony Reader in Classical Epigraphy, Dr Fowler, who was fond of repeating, as a kind of motto, 'Tell it not in Gath!' Next door to us, separated only by a wall, lived a profoundly learned scholar, the university librarian. He knew many languages, and pages of Dickens by heart, and sometimes we would hear him pacing up and down, reciting and laughing. A sweet, innocent child, really, a Dickensian character himself: one day, he was on the bus with my father, going to the university, and embarrassed him by loudly opining, 'You could say that the girls who serve in Woolworth's are the *intellectual scum of the earth*.' This academic-religious world had obscure prohibitions and rules. There was a historian who for some reason forbade his two slightly green-hued, fearsomely clever daughters from watching *The Forsyte Saga* on television; and a thrifty Professor of Divinity whose household had no television and who, according to my mother, always had sausages, never turkey, on Christmas Day – that family's fantastical drabness sealed in my childish mind by the information that he and his wife and three children exchanged only cotton handkerchiefs as presents. Our headmaster at the Durham Chorister School, also a clergy-man, had an elaborate system of mnemonics to help us with difficult Latin words. Whenever the word *unde* appeared in a text, he would suck on his pipe and intone, in Oxonian basso, 'Marks and Spencer, Marks and Spencer!' This was supposed to trigger, 'Where do you get your undies?' 'From Marks and Spencer.' And then lead us to the meaning of the word, which is: 'from where'. As you can see, I haven't forgotten it.

II

A recent editorial in the Brooklyn-based literary journal *n+1* inveighed against so-called 'World Literature'. In their opinion, post-colonial writing has lost its political bite and now fills its toothless face at the trough of global capitalism. *Midnight's Children* gave way, as it were, to the inoffensive Rushdie of *The Ground Beneath Her Feet*. The essay argued that World Literature should really be called Global Literature. It has its royalty, like Coetzee and Ondaatje, Mohsin Hamid and Kiran Desai; its prizes (the Nobel, the Man Booker International), its festivals (Jaipur, Hay) and its intellectual support system (the universities). The success of World Literature, said the editors, is a by-product of successful capitalism, and of a globalised aesthetic that prizes writers who, like Orhan Pamuk, Ma Jian and Haruki Murakami, are thought to have transcended local issues and acquired a 'universal relevance'.

It was hard not to share *n+1*'s derision, once its victim had been so tendentiously trussed. Who could possibly approve of this complacent, festival-haunting, unit-shifting, prize-winning monster? Who wouldn't choose instead, as the editors did, a 'thorny internationalism' over the 'smoothly global', untranslatable felicities over windy width – and Elena Ferrante over Kamila Shamsie? In the end, the journal was really making a wise case for well-written,

vital, challenging literature, full of sharp local particulari-
ties, wherever it turns up in the world; and so there was
inevitably something a bit random about the writers it
chose for its preferred canon of Thorny Internationalists:
Elena Ferrante, Kirill Medvedev, Samanth Subramanian,
Juan Villoro.

Perhaps, though, post-colonial literature hasn't only
morphed into a bloated World Lit. One of its new
branches may be a significant contemporary literature
that moves between, and powerfully treats, questions of
homelessness, displacement, emigration, voluntary or
economic migration and even flaneurial tourism; a literature that blurs the demarcations offered in 'Reflections
on Exile', because emigration itself has become more
complex, amorphous and widespread. The editors at *n+1*
inaudibly conceded as much in its editorial, when they
praised *Open City*, by Teju Cole, a Nigerian writer based
in New York City, whose first novel is narrated by a
young half-Nigerian, half-German psychiatry intern, and
which mixes elements of familiar post-coloniality with
W.G. Sebald's flaneurial émigré sensibility. Cole, it seems,
is approved of, but doesn't quite make the Thorny
Internationalist cut.

But to *Open City* could be added W.G. Sebald's work;
Patrick McGuiness's *Other People's Countries*; the Nigerian
novelist Taiye Selasi; Joseph O'Neill's *Netherland*, which
makes acute distinctions between the privileged economic
migration of the Dutch banker who narrates the novel and

the much less privileged immigration of the Trinidadian trickster who is the book's tragic hero; the work of the Bosnian-American writer, Aleksandar Hemon; Marilynne Robinson's *Home*; Mavis Gallant's short stories, written by a Canadian who spent most of her life in Paris; Zia Haider Rahman's formidable first novel, *In the Light of What We Know*; some of the writing of Geoff Dyer; the stories of Nam Le, a Vietnamese-born Australian; the fiction and essays of the Indian novelist Amit Chaudhuri.

The 'great movement of peoples that was to take place in the second half of the twentieth century' that V.S. Naipaul spoke of in *The Enigma of Arrival* was, as Naipaul put it, 'a movement between all the continents'. It could no longer be confined to a single paradigm (post-colonialism, internationalism, globalism, world litera-ture). The jet engine has probably had a greater impact than the Internet. It brings a Nigerian to New York, a Bosnian to Chicago, a Mexican to Berlin, an Australian to London, a German to Manchester. It brought one of *n+1*'s founding editors, Keith Gessen, as a little boy, from Russia to America in 1981, and now takes him back and forth between those countries (a liberty unknown to émigrés like Nabokov or Sergei Dovlatov).

Recall Lukács's phrase 'transcendental homelessness'. What I have been describing, both in my own life and the lives of others, is more like secular homelessness. It cannot claim the theological prestige of the transcendent. Perhaps it is not even homelessness; *homelooseness* (with an admixture of loss) might be the necessary neologism: in which the ties that might bind one to Home have been loosened, perhaps happily, perhaps unhappily, perhaps permanently, perhaps only temporarily. Clearly, this secular homelessness overlaps, at times, with the more established categories of emigration, exile and post-colonial movement. Just as clearly, it diverges from them at times. W.G. Sebald, a German writer who lived most of his adult life in England (and who was thus perhaps an emigrant, certainly an immigrant, but not exactly an émigré, nor an exile), had an exquisite sense of the varieties of not-belonging. He came to Manchester, from Germany, in the mid-1960s, as a graduate student. He returned, briefly, to Switzerland, and then came back to England in 1970, to take a lectureship at the University of East Anglia. The pattern of his own emigration is one of secular homelessness or homelooseness. He had the economic freedom to return to West Germany; and once he was well known, in the mid-1990s, he could have worked almost anywhere he wanted to.

Sebald was interested, however, not in his own wandering, but in an emigration and displacement closer to tragic or transcendental homelessness. In *The Emigrants*, he wrote about four such wanderers: Dr Henry Selwyn, a Lithuanian Jew who arrived in Britain at the beginning of the twentieth century, and who lived a life of stealthy masquerade as an English doctor, before committing suicide late in life; Paul Bereyter, a German who because of his part-Jewish ancestry was prohibited from teaching during the Third Reich, never recovered from this setback and later committed suicide; Sebald's great-uncle, Adelwarth, who arrived in America in the 1920s, worked as a servant for a wealthy family on Long Island, but ended up in a mental asylum in Ithaca, New York; and Max Ferber, a fictional character based on the painter Frank Auerbach, who left his parents behind in Germany in 1939, when he escaped for England.

When *The Emigrants* appeared in Michael Hulse's English translation, in 1996, it was often described as a book about four victims of the Holocaust, which it was not – only two of the emigrants are direct victims. Because the book is deeply invested in questions of fictionality, decipherment and archival witness – and because of the book's teasing photographs – it was also often assumed that these were fictional or fictionalised sketches. Almost the opposite is true. They are more like documentary life-studies; Sebald said in an interview that about 90 per cent of the photographs were 'what you would describe as authentic, i.e., they really did come out of the photo albums of the people described in those texts and are a direct testimony of the fact that these people did exist in that particular shape and form'. Sebald did indeed meet Dr Selwyn in 1970; Paul Bereyter was Sebald's primary-school teacher; his great-uncle Adelwarth immigrated to America in the 1920s; and Max Ferber's life was closely modelled on Frank Auerbach's.

None of this suggests that Sebald doesn't enrich the documentary evidence in all kinds of subtle, slippery, fictive ways. And one of the subtleties involves his relationship, as a kind of emigrant, with his subjects. Henry Selwyn and Max Ferber were, essentially, political refugees, from different waves of twentieth-century Jewish flight; Adelwarth was an economic immigrant; and Paul Bereyter became an inner emigrant, a post-war German survivor who, in the end, did not survive. And Sebald himself? His own emigration would seem to play out in a minor key, by comparison. Officially, he could return to his homeland whenever he wanted. But perhaps he had decided, for political reasons, that he could never go home again, could never return to a country whose unfinished post-war business had so disgusted him in the 1960s.

Sebald is a ghostly presence in *The Emigrants*. We are offered only glimpses of the German academic in England. Yet in another way, the author is strongly present, felt as a steady insistence in regulated hysteria. Who is this apparently well-established professor, so obsessed with the lives of his subjects that he crosses Europe or the Atlantic to interview their relatives, ransack their archives, frown over their photograph albums and follow their journeys? There is a beautiful moment in the first story, about Dr Henry Selwyn, when the text glances at Sebald's own, lesser homelessness, and then glances away, as if politely conceding its smaller claim on tragedy:

108

On one of these visits, Clara being away in town, Dr Selwyn and I had a long talk prompted by his asking whether I was ever homesick. I could not think of any adequate reply, but Dr Selwyn, after a pause for thought, confessed (no other word will do) that in recent years he had been beset by homesickness more and more.

Sebald then describes Dr Selwyn's homesickness for the village in Lithuania he had to leave at the age of seven. We hear about the horse-ride to the station, the train journey to Riga, the ship from Riga and the arrival in a broad river estuary:

All the emigrants had gathered on deck and were waiting for the Statue of Liberty to appear out of the drifting mist, since every one of them had booked a passage to Americum, as we called it. When we disembarked we were still in no doubt whatsoever that beneath our feet was the soil of the New World, of the Promised City of New York. But in fact, as we learnt some time later to our dismay (the ship having long since cast off again), we had gone ashore in London.

I find moving the way in which Sebald's homesickness becomes Selwyn's, is swallowed by the acuter claims of the larger narrative. We can only guess at the smothered

109

anguish in Sebald's primly painful aside, 'I could not think of any adequate reply.' There is also, perhaps, something touchingly estranged, unhoused even, about Sebald's language – this peculiar, reticent, antiquarian prose, in an English created by Michael Hulse and then strenuously worked over by the bilingual author.

Sebald seems to know the difference between homesickness and homelessness, between homelooseness and homelessness. If there is anguish, there is also discretion: how could my loss *adequately* compare with yours? Where exile is often marked by the absolutism of the separation, homelooseness is marked by a certain provisionality, a structure of departure and return that may not end. This is a powerful motif in the work of Aleksandar Hemon, who came to the States from Sarajevo, in 1992, only to discover that the siege of his home town prohibited his return. Hemon stayed in America, learned how to write a brilliant, Nabokovian English (a feat actually greater than Nabokov's because achieved at a phenomenal pace) and published his first book, *The Question of Bruno*, in 2000 (dedicated to his wife, and to Sarajevo). Once the Bosnian war was over, Hemon could presumably have returned to his native city. What had not been a choice became one; he decided to make himself into an American writer.

Hemon's work stages both his departure and return. In the novella *Blind Jozef Pronek & Dead Souls*, Pronek arrives in America on a student exchange programme.

Like Hemon, Pronek is from Sarajevo, is trapped by the war and stays in America. He finds the United States a bewildering, alienating place, full of vulgarity and ignorance. When, near the end of the story, he returns to Sarajevo, the reader expects him to stay. Though the city is terribly damaged, and familiar landmarks have disappeared, he seems to have come back to his 'true home' – where 'every place had a name, and everybody and everything in that place had a name, and you could never be nowhere, because there was something everywhere'. Sarajevo, it seems, is where names and things, words and referents, are primally united. He goes through his parents' apartment, touching everything:

> the clean, striped tablecloth; the radio, with seven ivory-colored buttons and a Donald Duck sticker; the grinning African masks; the carpets with intricate, yet familiar, geometric patterns, full of gashes, from under which the parquet was gone, burnt in the rusty iron stove in the corner; the demitasse, the coffee grinder, the spoons; Father's suits, damp, with shrapnel slashes . . .

But Jozef does not stay, and as the novella closes, we see him in Vienna airport, about to board a flight to America:

> He did not want to fly to Chicago. He imagined walking from Vienna to the Atlantic Ocean, and then hopping on a slow trans-Atlantic steamer. It would take a month

to get across the ocean, and he would be on the sea, land and borders nowhere to be found. Then he would see the Statue of Liberty and walk slowly to Chicago, stopping wherever he wished, talking to people, telling them stories about far-off lands, where people ate honey and pickles, where no one put ice in the water, where pigeons nested in pantries.

It's as if jet-flight is existentially shallow; a slower journey would enact the gravity and enormity of the transformation. Pronek returns to America, but must take his home with him, and must try to tell incomprehensible stories – pigeons in the pantries, honey and pickles – of that home to a people who readily confuse Bosnia with Slovakia, and write off the war as 'thousands of years of hatred'. And at the same time, he is making a new home in America. Or not quite: for he will stay in America, but will, it seems, never rid himself of the idea that putting ice in the water is a foolish superfluity. And like Sebald, though in a different register, Hemon writes a prose that does not sound smoothly native – a fractionally homeless prose. Like his master, Nabokov, he has the immigrant's love of puns, of finding buried meanings in words that have become flattened in English, like *vacuous* and *petrified*. One character has 'a sagely beard', another 'fenestral glasses'. Tea is described as 'limpid'.

Exile is acute, massive, transformative, but homelooseness, because it moves along its axis of departure and return, can be banal, welcome, necessary, continuous. There is the movement of the provincial to the metropolis, or the journey out of one social class into another. This was my mother's journey from Scotland to England, my father's journey from the working classes into the middle classes, my short drive from Durham to London. It is Ursula Brangwen's struggle for departure, in *The Rainbow*, when she quarrels with her parents about leaving her home in the Midlands and becoming a teacher in Kingston-upon-Thames – what her father calls 'dancing off to th'other side of London'.

Most of us have to leave home, at least once; there is the necessity to leave, the difficulty of returning and then, in later life as one's parents begin to falter, the necessity to return again. Secular homelessness, not the singular extremity of the exile or the chosenness of biblical diaspora, might be the inevitable ordinary state. Secular homelessness is not just what will always occur in Eden, but what should occur, again and again. There is a beautiful section at the end of Ismail Kadare's great novel, *Chronicle in Stone*, entitled 'Draft of a Memorial Plaque'. Kadare was born, in 1936, in the city of Gjirokastër, in southern Albania, but has spent much of his writing life in Paris. *Chronicle in Stone* is a joyful, comic tribute to the ancient native city he left behind. At the end of the book, Kadare directly addresses his home town: 'Often, striding along wide lighted boulevards in foreign cities, I somehow stumble in places where no one ever trips. Passersby turn in surprise, but I always know it's you. You emerge from the asphalt all of a sudden and then sink back down straight away.' It is Kadare's nicely humdrum version of the moment in Proust when Marcel stumbles on the uneven stones in the courtyard of the Guermantes, and memory opens itself up.

If it didn't trip you up, you wouldn't remember anything. For the émigré writer, returning to live in Gjirokastër is doubtless unimaginable, in rather the way that living in Paris must have seemed unimaginable when Kadare was a young man in Albania. But a life without stumbling is also unimaginable: perhaps to be in between two places, to be at home in neither, is the inevitable fallen state, almost as natural as being at home in one place.

III

Almost. But not quite. When I left England eighteen years ago, I didn't know then how strangely departure would obliterate return: how could I have known? It's one of time's lessons, and can only be learned temporally. What is peculiar, even a little bitter, about living for so many years away from the country of my birth is the slow revelation that I made a large choice many years ago that did not resemble a large choice at the time; that it has taken years for me to see this; and that this process of retrospective comprehension in fact constitutes a life – is indeed how life is lived. Freud has a wonderful word, 'afterwardness', which I need to borrow, even at the cost of kidnapping it from its very different context. To think about home and the departure from home, about not going home and no longer feeling able to go home, is to be filled with a remarkable sense of 'afterwardness': it is too late to do anything about it now, and too late to know what should have been done. And that may be all right.

My Scottish grandmother used to play a game, in which she entered the room with her hands behind her back. You had to guess which hand held a sweet, as she intoned: 'Which hand do you tak', the richt or the wrang?' When we were children, the decision seemed momentous: you *had* at all costs to avoid the disappointment of the empty 'wrang hand'.

Which did I choose?

Acknowledgements

THE FIRST THREE CHAPTERS of this book were written, in slightly different form, as the Mandel Lectures, delivered in April 2013 at the Mandel Center for the Humanities, Brandeis University. I am very grateful to the university, and to the Center's director, Professor Ramie Targoff, for asking me to give these talks. I am also grateful to Professor Michael Willrich, who was my warmly welcoming host. A version of the first chapter appeared in the *New Yorker*, and brief portions of Chapters Two and Three appeared in the *Michigan Quarterly Review* and *n+1*. I would like to thank the editors of those journals for their support.

The fourth chapter was first delivered as a lecture, too: at the British Museum, in February 2014, in a series run by the museum and the *London Review of Books*. It subsequently appeared in the *London Review of Books*. I am grateful to the Museum's director for the use of its superb auditorium, and deeply indebted to the *LRB*'s editor,

Mary-Kay Wilmers, for inviting me to give this lecture, and for being such a generous editor and host.

Mark Greif was kind enough to send me a copy of his essay, 'All There is to Use', before it was published; and Matthew Adams gave me – inadvertently – the passage from Nabokov's *Lectures on Literature*. I hope I can thank them without implying that they would necessarily agree with everything in this book.

Notes

Epigraph

'Art is the nearest thing to life': from 'The Natural History of German Life', in George Eliot, *Selected Essays, Poems, and Other Writings* (Penguin Classics, 1990), 110.

1

5 'Each person dies': 'Literature and the Right to Death', trans. Lydia Davis, in Maurice Blanchot, *The Work of Fire* (Stanford University Press, 1995), 337.

10 'the breasts becoming important': D.H. Lawrence, *The Rainbow* (Penguin Classics, 2007), 178.

10 'He was slender, and, to her': Lawrence, 421.

11 'everything is permitted': see Dostoevsky, Book Eleven of *The Brothers Karamazov.*

12 'To the artist, new experiences of "truth"': Thomas Mann, *Essays of Three Decades*, trans. H.T. Lowe-Porter (Knopf, 1976), 330.

14 as Coleridge does: Coleridge, *Biographia Literaria*, ed. Nigel Leask (Everyman/Dent, 1997), 293.

16 'Don't die, Señor': Cervantes, *Don Quixote*, trans. John Rutherford (Penguin Classics, 2000), 980.

16 'Our whole life is but a parenthesis': John Donne, 'Sermon Preached to the Countesse of Bedford, at Harrington House', 7 January 1620. Best available text is online, at BibleStudyTools.com (The Works of John Donne, Volume 4): http://www.biblestudytools.com/classics/the-works-of-john-donne-vol-4/sermon-cxi.html. Accessed 11 June 2014.

17 Walter Benjamin's argument: Walter Benjamin, 'The Storyteller', in *Illuminations*, trans. Harry Zohn (Fontana, 1973), 83–109.

19 '*Was*. We say *he is*': Thomas Bernhard, *The Loser*, trans. Jack Dawson (Vintage, 2006), 40.

19 Nabokov liked to point out: Vladimir Nabokov, *Strong Opinions* (Vintage, 1990), 93.

20 'In all Mr Biswas lived six years': V.S. Naipaul, *A House for Mr Biswas* (Vintage, 2001), 174.

21 'Well, this Fichte is lucky': Penelope Fitzgerald, *The Blue Flower* (Mariner Books, 1995), 80.

23 'An extraordinary notion came to the Freifrau Auguste': Fitzgerald, 161.

24 'At the end of the 1790s': Fitzgerald, 226.

26 The classical historian Robin Lane Fox: Robin Lane Fox, *The Unauthorized Version: Truth and Fiction in The Bible* (Knopf, 1992), 404: 'In the Old Testament there is only one accidental death: the baby which the prostitute before Solomon has smothered in her sleep; its death is incidental to the story of the king's judgement. Even a sickness is a punishment from God or the cue for deliberate acts of healing, carried out by men of God. For although God is not the active cause of everything, he is an ever-present agent and the world is his Creation.'

27 'A person's life consists': Italo Calvino, *Mr Palomar* (Vintage Classics, 1999), 111.

2

31 'a short, round-shouldered officer': Anton Chekhov, 'The Kiss', in *Early Stories*, trans. Patrick Miles and Harvey Pitcher (Oxford, 1994), 172.

37 'that great brilliant upper part': Henry Green, *Loving* (Penguin, 1978), 76.

38 'Why there's all those stories': Green, 79.

38 'D'you stand there': Green, 121.

40 the Scottish poet Robin Robertson: 'Crimond', in *Hill of Doors* (Picador, 2013), 63.

44 'The noxious, sour manure stench': Aleksandar Hemon, 'Exchange of Pleasant Words', in *The Question of Bruno: Stories* (Vintage, 2001), 111.

45 'To draw is to look': John Berger, *Berger on Drawing*, ed. Jim Savage (Occasional Press, 2005), 71.

46 'Juicy green leaves': Leo Tolstoy, *War and Peace*, trans. Richard Pevear and Larissa Volokhonsky (Knopf, 2007), 422. The passage appears in Volume II, Part Three, Chapter 3 of the novel.

46 'compact sea-lion skin': Jean-Paul Sartre, *Nausea*, trans. Robert Baldick (Penguin, 2000), 186.

48 'It was strange how all trees': Karl Ove Knausgaard, *My Struggle: Book Three*, trans. Don Bartlett (Archipelago, 2014), 80.

48 'big but light elbow': Saul Bellow, *Seize the Day* (Penguin, 1996), 100.

48 'They were awkward and the ball bounded high': Bellow, 107.

50 'drooping Victorian shoulders': 'Kangaroo', in D.H. Lawrence, *The Complete Poems* (Penguin, 1971), 393.

50 'dark, deflated tennis balls': in Aleksandar Hemon, *The Question of Bruno: Stories* (Vintage, 2001), 89

50 'like a moral owl': 'Letter to N.Y.', in Elizabeth Bishop, *The Complete Poems* (The Hogarth Press, 1984), 80.

50 'flinching': Adam Foulds, *The Quickening Maze* (Penguin, 2010), 51.

50 Nabokov's great defamiliarising joke: Vladimir Nabokov, *Pnin* (Penguin, 1960), 52–3: 'until workmen came and started to drill holes in the street – Brainpan

Street, Pningrad – and patch them up again, and this went on and on, in fits of shivering black zigzags and stunned pauses, for weeks, and it did not seem likely they would ever find again the precious tool they had entombed by mistake'.

53 'becoming smaller and smaller': Karl Ove Knausgaard, *My Struggle: Book Three*, trans. Don Bartlett (Archipelago, 2012), 386.

55 'I looked in at McKern': 'Something to Remember Me By', in Saul Bellow, *Collected Stories* (Penguin, 2001), 435.

56 'To minor authors': Vladimir Nabokov, *Lectures on Literature* (Harcourt Brace, 1980), 2.

57 'By that quiver of pleasure': 'Of Cruelty', in Michel de Montaigne, *The Complete Works*, trans. Donald M. Frame (Everyman's Library, 2003), 375.

57 'feelers bent': Saul Bellow, *Herzog* (Penguin, 1965), 113.

58 'swiping around for signs of its own life': Rachel Kushner, *The Flamethrowers* (Scribner, 2013), 56.

58 'felt the life of perished things': in Marilynne Robinson, *Housekeeping* (Picador, 2004), 124.

58 'a fact that allows us': *ibid*, p. 194

58 'attentiveness': Walter Benjamin and Theodor Adorno, *The Complete Correspondence, 1928–1940* (Polity, 2003), 66–71.

59 'if the thought really yielded to the object': Theodor Adorno, *Negative Dialectics* (Continuum, 1973), 27–8.

3

64 'With a totally non-literary working-class back-ground': *Novels and Novelists: A Guide to the World of Fiction*, ed. Martin Seymour-Smith (Windward Books/W.H. Smith, 1980), 84–5. All subsequent references are to this edition.

73 who coined the term 'practical criticism': see Coleridge, *Biographia Literaria*, Chapter 15, 186: 'In the application of these principles to purposes of practical criticism . . . I have endeavoured to discover what the qualities in a poem are . . .'

74 'The main ideal of criticism': Mark Greif, 'All There is to Use', in *The Critical Pulse: Thirty-Six Credos by Contemporary Critics*, ed. Heather Steffen and Jeffrey J. Williams (Columbia University Press, 2012), 237–44.

74 'The mere understanding': see 'On the Knocking at the Gate in *Macbeth*', in Thomas De Quincey, *On Murder* (Oxford University Press, 2006), 3–7.

78 When the great short-story writer Eudora Welty: Eudora Welty, *The Eye of the Story* (Vintage, 1990), 139.

79 When Coleridge writes of Swift: *Specimens of the Table Talk of the late Samuel Taylor Coleridge*, Volume 1 (John Murray, 1835), 178.

79 when Henry James says: 'Honoré de Balzac', in Henry James, *The Critical Muse: Selected Literary Criticism*, ed. Roger Gard (Penguin, 1987), 352. The Balzac

essay first appeared in 1902. In an earlier essay, on Flaubert, from 1893, James gave the phrase, as it were, a trial run: 'he [Flaubert] appears truly to have been made of the very stuff of a Benedictine' (*The Critical Muse*, 308). Second time lucky.

79 when Pritchett laments: 'Fordie', in V.S. Pritchett, *The Complete Essays* (Chatto & Windus, 1991), 565.

80 a 'talent for metaphor': see Ted Cohen, *Thinking of Others: On the Talent for Metaphor* (Princeton University Press, 2008). All subsequent references are to this edition.

83 'All that he had done again and again in his books': Virginia Woolf, *Roger Fry: A Biography* (Harvest/ Harcourt, 1976), 262–3.

4

91 Herodotus says that the Scythians: Herodotus, *The History*, trans. David Grene (University of Chicago Press, 1987), 298.

92 'Exile is strangely compelling to think about': Edward Said, *Reflections on Exile and Other Essays* (Harvard University Press, 2001), 173.

95 'There was no reason for me to be born Belgian': Patrick McGuinness, *Other People's Countries: A Journey into Memory* (Jonathan Cape, 2014), 144.

96 'The rudeness, the lies': Sergei Dovlatov, *A Foreign Woman* (Grove Press, 1991), 94.

96 I once saw, in Germany: at the Deutsches Literatur-archiv, in the town of Marbach am Neckar.

99 'The exile's new world': Said, 181.

99 'changed itself to past': 'MCMXIV', in Philip Larkin, *Collected Poems* (Faber & Faber, 2003), 99.

103 A recent editorial: see *n+1*, Issue 17, Fall 2013.

105 'great movement of peoples': V.S. Naipaul, *The Enigma of Arrival* (Vintage, 1988), 141: 'Because in London I was at the beginning of that great movement of peoples that was to take place in the second half of the twentieth century – a movement and a cultural mixing greater than the peopling of the United States, which was essentially a movement of Europeans to the New World.'

107 Sebald said in an interview: James Wood, 'An Interview with W.G. Sebald', *Brick* 59, Spring, 1998, 25. The interview, which took place in New York City in 1997, can also be found in *The New Brick Reader*, ed. Tara Quinn (House of Anansi Press, 2013), 8–16.

109 'On one of these visits': W.G. Sebald, *The Emigrants*, trans. Michael Hulse (New Directions, 1996), 18–19.

109 'All the emigrants': Sebald, 19.

111 'every place had a name': Hemon, 201.

111 'the clean, striped tablecloth': Hemon, 203.

111 'He did not want to fly to Chicago': Hemon, 209.

113 'dancing off to th'other side of London': Lawrence, 339.

113 'Often, striding along wide lighted boulevards': Ismail

Kadare, *Chronicle in Stone*, trans. Arshi Pipa, revised by David Bellos (Canongate, 2011), 301.

115 'afterwardness': see especially 'Notes on Afterwardness', in Jean Laplanche, *Essays on Otherness* (London, 1999).

Index